Beams
of Light
Piercing
the
Storm

"For I know the plans I have for you, declares the Lord, plans for welfare and not for evil, to give you a future and a hope."

Jeremiah 29:11 (ESV)

Beams of Light Piercing the Storm

Finding Hope in the Midst of Tragedy and Uncertainty

Kimberly Williams

Contributing Author
Caleb Williams

Published by
Graceful Script

Second Printing: January 2015

Published by Graceful Script

ISBN: 978-0-69-234154-4

Cover design by GaBrielle Boyd

Published and printed in the United States of America

Dedication

CR

To my parents, Keith and Veronica Lierman

Throughout my childhood, you modeled living a life
trusting in the Lord, regardless of circumstance. Your
faithfulness in teaching me to trust in the Lord set a
foundation giving me the strength to endure through
trials. Throughout my greatest trial, your continued
reminders to trust in Jesus provided the encouragement
for me to keep going from day to day and to recognize the
beams of light piercing my storm.

Contents

CR

Preface

CR

Monday June 20, 2005

I grabbed my vacuum to finish a few chores before hopping into the shower. My husband and I looked forward to dinner plans for our 18th wedding anniversary.

As I vacuumed, the thought crossed my mind that it was about time to go to the river and pick up Caleb. My cell phone rang around 3:30 p.m. On the other end of the line, a friend asked if I knew Caleb was at the river. I knew. I had dropped him off around 1:00 p.m. The next words relayed that Caleb had been hurt. Our friend didn't know what exactly had happened, but the aid cars had been called. I left my other two teen-age children, Josh and Sarah, at home, since I didn't know exactly what was happening, and I drove to the river.

The drive to the river took only about ten minutes. I guessed that Caleb had probably hurt a leg or something similar, which would mean missing basketball nationals in Tennessee in two weeks. I expected "an" aid car, but when I got to the river, there were eight or more aid cars – fire, police, and ambulance. Instantly, my body tensed with worry. Although I was still recovering from a surgery two weeks before, I jogged down to the river. From the shore I could see several people on a small island. They surrounded Caleb, who was out of sight. I could hear paramedics relaying messages on their radios. I heard bits and pieces, but understood that Caleb was in and out of consciousness and not very responsive. The airlift helicopter for Harborview Medical Center was en route. Many people watched from the riverbank, but no one knew exactly how badly he was hurt.

The next year was filled with pain, fear, uncertainty, and most definitely, miracles. As I have written and rewritten this account, it seems impossible to truly express the emotions of the event. At first I felt shock... then fear and grief... uncertainty... despair... helplessness... but also hope... trust in God... moments of joy. Words seem inadequate to relate the events. Even from the moment Caleb hit the rocks, God was present and miracles began happening.

I have written this account so that Caleb, our family, our friends, and anyone who may read it will see the hand of God in a miraculous healing and in the life of Caleb. Caleb should not be functioning as he is today. But I believe, and did believe throughout the process, that God saved Caleb for a purpose. I may never know all the purpose in this event. I do see many ways that God used this in the lives of our family, our community, and people we will never even meet. God's ways are so much bigger than I am. This story shares an account of God sending beams of light to pierce our storm right from the moment Caleb fell...

Chapter 1

The Walls Crash In

CR

Even during my pregnancy, Caleb showed signs of activity. In his younger years, I would tell him that he started playing soccer even before his birth. As he grew, he showed unusual athletic abilities. He began riding a two-wheel bike at age three. By age four, he informed us that he needed a "trick" bike. I believed him because he loved to hold onto the handlebars and stand up on the seat as he coasted. Also by age three, he dribbled a regular sized basketball whenever we walked to the park or mall near our home. He loved basketball and played on our little kid hoop in the hallway or on a portable hoop in the driveway. He watched professional games and imitated players. Michael Jordan was a favorite... he was every kid's favorite then. Caleb asked to record games, and then he would take the VCR remote and watch games to study the players, especially Jordan. Caleb watched a move, hit rewind four or five times to study it, then practiced the same move on our little kid hoop. Now this process may seem normal for a middle or high school aged youth, but Caleb was four years old. Blended with his relentless on-the-go nature emerged an extroverted comic who loved attention. He modeled empty ice cream bowls on his head or walked into walls with a bucket on his head. He loved to laugh and to make us laugh. He was the kind of fearless kid who needs constant monitoring because, as soon as I turned my back, he jumped into the deep end of the pool without any floaties. He was a good-natured, energetic, adventurous, daring bundle of enthusiasm rushing out to live every moment to its fullest.

As time went on, his love for basketball continued. As a first grader, he played in a league with third and fourth graders... and he could compete. In third grade, he joined his brother, Josh, on a fifth grade team. At this young age, he competed against fifth and sixth grade boys, and he loved it. During middle school years, he began traveling with his basketball teams, and our family trekked to tournaments in Arizona, Florida, California, Nevada, and various regions in Washington.

Throughout 7th-9th grade, Caleb played against some serious talent from various parts of the country... California, New York, Texas, Philadelphia. Many opposing teams held positions of notoriety in the basketball world. Being a point guard, he normally matched up on defense against other point guards. Some of the guards he played against were lightening quick and very talented... and they knew it. But Caleb *loved* the challenge of frustrating other point guards. He was tenacious on defense, and once he got under the skin of an opponent, he played like a shark pursuing wounded prey. Once the opponent showed "fear", Caleb turned up the intensity even more.

Other players loved to play with Caleb. He had noticeable talent, but the real draw was Caleb's ability to bring out the best in each of his teammates. He read the floor and game situations so well that he could hit anyone on the court with a pass right where it was needed – regardless of that person's skill level. He played no favorites on the court. Teammates learned that if they worked to get open, Caleb could, and would, get them the ball. Few teammates felt threatened by Caleb's skills because he worked to help *them* shine on the court. Josh loved playing with Caleb, and being brothers, the two boys read and anticipated each other well on the court. Coach Andy (Dad), Sarah, and I loved watching Caleb play. Viewing his creative performance on the court was more like observing an artist than an athlete. As coach, Andy would receive comments from opposing coaches, "Number 32 (Caleb) passes too much... you need to tell that kid to shoot more." While these observations were intended as compliments to Caleb, such remarks never changed Caleb's play or attitude on the court. Through Andy's coaching and Caleb's own understanding of the game, Caleb grew into a true point guard. As the "floor general", he displayed uncanny court awareness and unselfish play.

By Caleb's freshman year in high school, other coaches were noticing. Several times at regional or national tournaments, opposing coaches would approach Caleb after a game and confirm to him that he had played a key role in defeating their team. A local scout maintained a website highlighting local talent and had ranked Caleb as the second strongest freshman point guard in the Pacific Northwest (Washington, Oregon, and Idaho). During seven years of his competitive basketball, Caleb played in forty-four league or tournament championships, and his team won thirty-four of those championship games. Caleb believed he could play with anyone who stepped onto the court, and the way he played exposed that obvious confidence. It looked like Caleb may have a bright future and a substantial college scholarship.

Now, many kids in this position can become really difficult to like as the ego takes over. But Caleb still enjoyed close reciprocal relationships with his peers. He loved people and people loved him; he felt at home in almost any social situation. We were clear with him that his grades came ahead of basketball, which encouraged Caleb to work hard in school. He loved the game too much to let poor grades hurt his chances of playing. By the end of his freshman year, he was on the honor roll, very popular with his classmates, and looking at playing college basketball. But change lurked right around the corner...

On June 20, 2005, a remarkably beautiful day for the Western Cascades, we enjoyed sunny, clear skies and eighty degree temperatures. Finals week at Mount Si High School meant half days of school for this last week before summer break. Everyone anticipated the excitement of the end of the school year, and the bright weather magnified the enthusiasm. Living near mountains, rivers, and lakes means summer weather in our part of the country comes with outdoor activities.

Caleb asked to go to the river with some friends, and after school, I dropped him to join his friends at one of the popular river spots, Blue Hole. Although I should have checked out the location before giving Caleb permission to go, I was naïve to the dangers of this area. At the river, kids had been swimming and swinging off a rope swing which hung on the shore directly above a rock face. From the rope, a person would swing about twenty feet before flying past the rocks to drop into the water. People who did not let go of the rope at the right time found themselves swinging over the rock face. As one of Caleb's friends swung out, she became frightened and didn't let go over the river. Unable to safely return to shore, she continued swinging over the rocks, so Caleb went to help her. Grabbing her with one hand and the rope with the other, he returned her to shore safely. As the girl dropped off the rope and Caleb continued to hold the rope with one hand, the momentum pulled Caleb over the rocks toward the river. Years later, I learned that although only one hand grasped the rope, Caleb managed to hang on and was swinging back toward the shore. Several of his friends thought he might make it back to shore, but he lost his grip and slipped off. He dropped onto the rocks with impact on his left arm and the left side of his face. Falling somewhere between fifteen and twenty-five feet, Caleb literally bounced off the rocks and into the river. Immediately, two friends dove into the river to pull Caleb to the surface. Blake was first into the river, and he dove down to find Caleb. At first he could not see Caleb, but then he spotted movement. Blake reached for the movement, grabbed Caleb by the hair, and pulled him up toward the surface. Justin helped Blake and the two boys hauled Caleb toward the shore.

Two other friends, Wes and Ben, dove in to help. The four boys managed to drag Caleb through the water to a small ledge in the rocks on the less accessible side of the river. Current was swift at this point, and the boys feared they might lose Caleb in the current if they tried to pull him across to level ground on the other side of the river. While another friend, Josh, called 911, the boys secured Caleb in the rock shelf, keeping his body in the water and his head above the surface. At one point, Blake had to submerge underneath Caleb and stand on the river bed to keep Caleb afloat. The boys continued to listen for breathing and to keep the airway clear. Caleb actually stopped breathing three times, so the boys revived him by yelling at him to stay with them and to breathe.

The first rescuers on the scene lacked authority to cross the river and help. While the initial 911 response team waited for the river rescue team, Justin, Blake, and Wes continued to hold Caleb in the water while Ben swam back and forth across the river transferring messages from the rescue aid team to the boys holding Caleb. This routine lasted forty-five minutes until the river rescue team arrived with a raft to stabilize Caleb and float him up to a calm stretch of river in order to cross the flow. By the time I arrived, Caleb lay on a small island between the two river banks. Trees and brush blocked my view, but I could hear the radio contact between the helicopter staff and the police on the ground. Eventually, the pilot located the site by following the news helicopters already above the scene. The rescue helicopter landed on the island, but I still could not see Caleb.

It was difficult to get any real information at this point. I could hear bits and pieces of the radio communication between the rescue personnel... I gathered that Caleb was unconscious, but he seemed to be breathing. Only a few minutes after I arrived on the scene, the rescue helicopter left to airlift Caleb to Harborview Medical Center in Seattle. A friend, George, offered to drive me to the hospital, and I called Andy and filled him in as much as possible.

Harborview Medical Center is a trauma center in a busy, downtown area of Seattle. As in any big city trauma center, Harborview staff members treat many difficult cases... gunshot victims, accident victims, burn victims, those with substance abuse, and people with no other place to go. This was not the kind of emergency room I had visited in my suburban life. Suburban hospitals offered comfortable stuffed chairs on carpeted floors. Fish tanks of tropical fish and tasteful artwork provided a pleasant atmosphere in those emergency rooms. The scene I entered felt more like a movie set than like any reality I had confronted before. The large room was packed with chairs – most of them occupied by suffering people. The sterile, cold ER had stark walls and old tile floors. There was nothing pleasant about this atmosphere. Twenty or thirty people sat waiting to receive treatment... and yet, Andy was already at a registration table providing information for Caleb. Almost as soon as I reached Andy, a social worker approached us. He told us Caleb had been intubated and CPR had been necessary during transport, and now Caleb was being examined and stabilized. We were assigned a special, private waiting room. This certainly indicated a sign of what we were about to face. In this crowded emergency room, we were rushed to the front of the line, provided a personal counselor, and sent to a private family waiting room... the hospital team expected the worst.

Within only a few minutes, we were escorted to see Caleb. He looked very beat up. His left eye was swollen like a purple golf ball. He had a breathing tube taped into his mouth and was on a respirator. His body became spastic and shook from hypothermia. And he was unconscious. After only a few moments with Caleb, we were taken back to the private waiting room while Caleb was moved to Intensive Care.

News of the accident spread quickly through our small community. Josh and Sarah received numerous calls from concerned friends, and people from our church quickly sent out the plea for prayer. Our pastor, Walt, arrived at Harborview, and as he joined us in our private waiting room, we grabbed cell phones to call family. I called my parents and calmly told them what had happened, but when Andy called his father, he struggled to get the words out. I calmly took the phone from Andy and told my father-in-law the news. I spoke with little emotion... completely robotic.

Moving to the cafeteria, we waited with George and Pastor Walt to hear news about the neurological exam. After some time, a neurosurgeon came to talk with us. The news was grim. Caleb was in a coma, and they did not know how extensive the brain damage was. There was no assurance Caleb would even live through the night. Even if Caleb did survive, the neurologist could not really say when, or even if, he would come out of the coma. However, at this point, we faced no immediate need to surgically relieve any brain pressure. The one hopeful piece of information was that Caleb did not need surgery to open up the skull and relieve pressure. The next seventy-two hours were important because if Caleb awoke within that time span, it would indicate minimal brain damage. Caleb's youth stood on his side, but we heard no real assurances or hope at that point.

I listened with no emotion. I perceived the words, but they washed past me as if I was having an out-of-body experience. Grasping the fact that we could really lose Caleb was more than I could process.

After hearing the neurology update, my concerned shifted to Dennae – the girl Caleb had saved. I expected that she blamed herself and probably felt fearful of our anger; however, I truly experienced no anger toward her. Throughout the whole ordeal, my primary feeling for her was compassion... I felt compelled to reassure her. As I spoke with her on the phone, she asked about Caleb's condition. I knew she wanted to hear that Caleb was okay, but sadly, I could give her no assurances. I could only relay my concern and compassion for her.

Throughout the initial hours of receiving the prognosis, I shed no tears and suffered no real panic... my manner was professional and matter-of-fact. At the time, I thought I was handling things exceptionally well, but of course, I was unknowingly in complete shock. Caleb was transported to ICU, and we waited for more news. Several people came to the hospital to wait and to pray with us. Perhaps six or seven hours after arriving at the hospital, the enormity of the situation started to sink in. I suddenly began to cry and to realize how completely powerless we were to do anything to help Caleb.

In ICU, the team managed to insert a brain pressure monitor into Caleb's skull, but an equipment malfunction prevented the monitor from receiving accurate readings. Waiting for updates from "simple" procedures like this seemed to take significant time. Eventually, the doctors told us we needed to go home and get some rest. We were specifically told we were in for "a long road" and we would need our strength. At 1:00 a.m., we walked out to our car and headed home.

Ten hours had passed since Caleb had slipped off the rope... those ten hours sent us onto a path we could never have expected nor properly prepared for. And yet, we are people of faith. How do people of faith cope with tragedy such as this? Where was God in this accident? From the very beginning, I knew I could not survive this without my faith. Odd as it may sound, neither Andy nor I ever felt angry with or abandoned by God. I began to look for the ways He was showing us His presence even in the face of the tragedy.

There were many ways I could see Him directing the situation even before Caleb hit the rocks.... Justin and Blake (the two who had pulled Caleb out of the water) arrived at the river only moments before Caleb sunk into the water. Before their arrival, the group at the river was mainly young girls. Justin and Blake were both athletic and had the strength needed to pull Caleb out of the strong current. It is possible that no one else previously at the river would have been able to pull him out quickly enough to save him. Even the fact that Caleb survived the fall at all was miraculous; he fell a significant distance and the impact alone could have killed him. Since he did sink into a river that had swift current and undertow, he could have drowned before anyone was able to pull him out of the water. Wes (the third boy holding Caleb in the river) had been through CPR and first aid training. Either because of the impact or because of swallowing water, Caleb vomited in his unconscious state. Wes kept a cool head and cleared Caleb's airway. He also had the foresight to yell at Caleb when breathing stopped three times. Somehow, Wes communicated with the subconscious part of Caleb's brain, and Caleb never stopped breathing for more than a short moment each time. Although we felt disbelief that the rescue teams did not enter the water and let three freshman boys take the responsibility to secure Caleb for forty-five minutes, that fact may have saved Caleb's life. His head trauma was severe. It was a sunny, eighty degree day. If Caleb had been pulled out of the river onto the shore for the forty-five minutes it took for airlift to arrive, his brain would almost certainly have continued to swell. The swelling alone could have caused death before he even arrived at Harborview. Being in the river, icy with spring run-off, effectively kept Caleb – and his brain – in a huge ice pack. His brain pressure never elevated to an unmanageable level. In fact, after the initial impact, his brain pressure and brain hemorrhaging never worsened.

Even from the first day of our trial, I knew that all these factors could not be woven together simply by chance. Surviving this ordeal required me to trust that God loved Caleb, loved us, and directed a bigger plan than what I could see. Faith and trust... easy to say, not easy to live. I had seen close family and friends live through tough situations... loss of a child, cancer, severe handicap, divorce. At this moment, I faced the most agonizing situation I have ever faced. And yet, I did not feel anger at or abandonment by God. I felt like Peter when he saw others walking away from Jesus,

"'Lord, to whom shall we go? You have the words of eternal life'" (John 6:68 ESV).

I had *no* other place to turn. Of course, I would face times when this trust would be rattled and fear would leave me curled up in a heap on the floor. But surviving this trial called for me to lift my head and look to the only source of hope available to me. I was *compelled* to trust God because I had nothing else left to trust.

Deliverance

"The righteous cry, and the Lord hears and delivers them out of all their troubles. The Lord is near to the brokenhearted, and saves those who are crushed in spirit" Psalm 34:17-18 (NASB).

What does deliverance look like... does it mean we get our way? What if we don't get our way? Where was God when this all happened? Caleb was not a "bad" kid. Certainly, he pushed boundaries as any teen does, but overall, he rarely got into deep trouble. He worked hard in school and accomplished almost a 4.0 grade-point. School was not easy for Caleb... he struggled to overcome learning challenges as a child. His grades were due to persistence and determination to surpass weaknesses and accomplish a goal. He pushed himself hard in his sport of basketball. Some said he was gifted – he was. But every talented individual who really excels in his/her talent works too. So where was God when a "good" kid was left at death's doorstep?

God was there from the time before the fall and He never left... but He may not have been there in the way we expected. We might have expected that He would have maintained Caleb's hold on the rope until he reached the shore... maybe a broken bone or two, but minimal injury. We might have expected that He would quickly and miraculously heal the brain damage from the impact. Certainly He is capable, so why not do so for a "good" kid? I never doubted that God *could* have done any of these things... but He chose not to. So where does that leave me? Did He abandon Caleb and us? If I believe He does not abandon us, which is what I did and do believe, then what is the answer? Sometimes God is not a lightning flash type of healer... sometimes His plan is slow and subtle. But He is not taken by surprise! He does have a plan, and He is not out on some other errand when suffering happens... He is intimately involved in the process. Am I willing to look for Him? He appeared in many ways... I just had to be open to ways I did not expect...

- Blake and Justin arrived at the river only moments before Caleb fell

- Wes had been through CPR/First Aid training and reacted quickly

- Caleb was not killed on impact

- Caleb was not swept away or pulled under by undertow

- Caleb stopped breathing three times while waiting for aid, but resumed breathing and was still alive when aid arrived

- The spring run-off water kept his brain in a giant "ice pack" which prevented excessive swelling

Yes, God was there. He was just there in a way different from my expectations.

Chapter 2

Life or Death: the First Week

☙

On Tuesday, June 21, the pressure monitor was in and functioning. Caleb's brain pressure seemed to fluctuate between about twenty and twenty-five units. The break-point was twenty-five units. Any time the pressure rose to twenty-five for more than a few seconds, nurses administered medication to stabilize the pressure. The goal was to reach a point where Caleb's brain could stabilize itself at or below fifteen units. This would be an indicator that we were past the point of possible additional brain damage due to elevated brain pressure. Again, I saw God's sustaining hand throughout the next week as the pressure remained stable with minimal administration of medication. Although the pressure pushed that twenty-five unit margin, Caleb never needed surgery to relieve skull pressure. By the end of the first week, brain pressure leveled out, and the monitor was removed.

Also on that Tuesday afternoon, we met with a Neurologist and received the first results of the tests and evaluations. The information was still imprecise, but it did give us a little more insight into what we were facing. We learned that the bleeds in Caleb's brain were scattered throughout the brain. His impact caused a diffuse axonal injury, which meant that the tiny neuro connections throughout the brain had suffered sheering effects, and the tiny connecting fibers between axons had been damaged or broken. A simplistic explanation of axons is that they are the fiber extensions that project from a nerve cell body and conduct electrical impulses to carry neurological signals throughout the brain and spinal tissue. For Caleb, areas of axon damage showed up on MRI and CAT scans as black areas where internal bleeding had occurred. Damage extent from this type of injury cannot be fully seen with current medical technology. The dark areas of bleeding can be seen, but whether fibers are completely or partially severed cannot be seen. The scans of Caleb's brain looked like tiny chocolate chips were sprinkled throughout the brain. In some regions, the bleeds were much larger. Although multiple bleeds were visible, the diagnosis resulted more from assessment of the practical effects of the injury. We were told that recovery for people who suffer this severity of injury may range from full recovery to no recovery at all. The medical staff reiterated that youth was on Caleb's side... but again... sometimes a healthy youngster does not recover even when it appears he should. We really had no answers for what to expect. Caleb did have a slight case of pneumonia from inhaling fluids, but the lung fluid was minimal and the pneumonia was really of little concern as it was treated with antibiotics. The real issue we faced was a severe Traumatic Brain Injury (TBI).

Over the next few days, several tests eliminated the concern of other injury. Doctors determined that there was no spinal cord injury which had been a real concern due to the height from which Caleb fell. His eyes were examined as well since there are multiple cranial nerves that send signals back and forth between the eyes and the brain. This was another important test to determine the extent of injury. Caleb's eyes showed good response which indicated that he would not lose sight due to the brain injury. He did have fractures in his nose and cheek, but both healed without need for manipulation. The left arm was also fractured but posed minimal concern. Each time, as more test results came in, the word was that he was strong and healthy except for the brain injury. The brain injury was not to be minimized, but considering what could have happened, we saw God's hand shielding Caleb from additional injury and complications.

Caleb was in the ICU for six days. During that time, he had *many* visitors. Each day I would arrive at the hospital between 10:00 a.m. and 11:00 a.m. Since Caleb was in the ICU, he could only have visitors when they were accompanied by a family member. Each day as I arrived, there were already several people, mostly Caleb's teen-age friends, waiting to see him. I would escort three or four friends at a time so they could see Caleb. These visits were often intense. Some friends were able to talk and let Caleb hear their voices, while others could only stand and watch with pained, even fearful, eyes. A few friends even collapsed and needed assistance to walk back to the waiting room. But every visit was welcomed. Strangely, these visits helped me survive each day. I rarely cried at the hospital because I took on a different role there. My nurturing attributes kicked in, and I spent most days reassuring and encouraging friends. I was amazed by these friends... Caleb looked horrible. He had multiple tubes in his body, was completely unresponsive, and to the common on-looker, did not look like he would make it. And yet the friends continued to stream into the ICU, day after day. By mid-week, I was escorting twenty to thirty visitors per day, every day. Most of these students returned three or four times during the week. Eventually, I had to ask the students to keep their visits between the hours of 11:00 a.m. and 7:00 p.m. so I could take family and other adult friends in to see Caleb in the evenings! Imagine – I had to "schedule" Caleb's visitors!

Some visits were especially difficult to experience. The night after the accident, the whole varsity basketball team – Caleb's team – came to visit. Not only were the boys there, but most of the parents and coaches came too. Strong, capable, athletic boys filed into the ICU in small groups to see Caleb. Even though he was the youngest player on the team, he was a floor leader and one who worked to make everyone else on the team a better player. Now he was down... and the reality of "one of their own" being down left them with somber faces and bewildered eyes.

Another difficult visit was the first time Blake, Justin, Wes, and Ben came. Most of these four who had been in the river to save Caleb were experiencing terrible

nightmares about the experience. I could relate to that...
I was having nightmares of Caleb falling from the rope. I
had not even been there to actually see the fall, but I
could picture it vividly in my dreams. How much more
these boys must have experienced. As each boy came, I
hugged him and told him that he was a hero to me. They
said, "Caleb would have done the same for us." But I
knew I would never forget these boys who had saved my
son.

Yet another apprehensive visitor was Dennae (the
girl Caleb rescued) who came that first week as well.
Shaking and pale, she sat in the waiting room not sure
she could face the image of Caleb in the ICU. I hugged
her and prayed into her ear so that only she could hear.
I thanked God that she was not in a bed next to Caleb,
and I prayed that she would have peace. She managed to
go into the ICU and to return other times to see him, but
that whole summer would be an agonizing time for her.

Each of these visitors was truly a blessing. The
medical staff had informed us that little is known about
the response of coma patients. There is research to
suggest that the subconscious brain can hear voices in
the room, even though voices may not be detected
consciously. For this reason, we kept everything positive
around Caleb. We never talked about what *might* be the
end result of his injury. We always encouraged him to
stay strong and fight to get better. For visitors, this meant
that we asked them not to cry in Caleb's room. Some
visitors could only stay a few minutes because they could
not hold in the intense emotion. But every visitor was
understanding and wanted to be positive around Caleb.
And as the days and weeks went on, the comfort level
increased as these very young teens talked, joked, held
Caleb's arm, and kept coming back. They were just like
any other sophomore students, nothing special about
them... and yet they were extraordinary. Before the end
of the first week these youth had organized prayer
sessions outside their high school, organized fund-raisers
to raise money for Caleb's medical expenses, brought
multiple cards for me to read to Caleb, and organized a

cleaning/yard work crew to help us at home for the rest of the summer. They faithfully visited him for weeks, from the last day of their freshman year well into the fall of their sophomore year. They showed surprising maturity and faithfulness.

These students came day after day and then went home. Their parents tried to help them cope as best they could. Even though Caleb lay in a hospital bed, Andy and I faced additional parental roles as well. Not only did we have to cope with Caleb's situation each day, but we wanted to be support for our two other children.

Josh did not need much support from us. Perhaps reversing roles, Josh became more of a support for me. Josh is gifted with the perfect personality for crisis situations. Very little rattles him. He has the ability to step back and logically assess the current situation without strong reaction to unknown outcomes that *might* occur. He could handle it when I just needed to cry and give him, my son, a hug. That stability seeped out and provided something solid for me to lean on.

Sarah had a much more difficult time with the reality of the accident. She was finishing her 7th grade year the week of the accident. Caleb was hurt on a Monday. Sarah stayed with friends on Tuesday and did not go to school. But Wednesday was the last day of the school year, and Sarah wanted to go for the half day. So she did go. That night while I was still at the hospital, she called my cell phone. As soon as I answered, she blurted, "What's going on!?" She sounded angry. Confused, I asked her what she meant. Many rumors surfaced around the school that day, and it was scaring her. One rumor was that *Andy* said Caleb might die. Other people stated Caleb might be "retarded", unable to walk, or unable to talk. Although these students had no idea what the real situation was, they offered their "knowledge" to Sarah. She thought we were hiding the reality of the situation from her. I explained that we didn't know what would happen. Yes, Caleb was badly hurt, but we did not know yet whether he would have permanent brain damage, trouble walking, or any other outcome. We were still waiting to see what would happen; there might be serious problems, but we still did not know. She did calm down, but we decided that she needed to come see Caleb for herself.

The next day, which was three days after the accident, some friends brought Sarah to see Caleb. We tried to warn Sarah that he looked pretty bad and that if she needed to leave, she could leave at any time. So we took her into the ICU to see him. She lasted only a few seconds before she started to cry. We took her out into the waiting room and she sobbed. It was so much for her to absorb. I really didn't know how to help her... this was a reality I could not fix or change. She did not want to go back in that day, and she stayed at the hospital only a short time. The emotional strain of this was intense for Sarah. We kept her busy with friends. As long as she could have diversion, she could cope with the stress of the situation. She hardly slept at home for a five week period. When she did stay at home, she couldn't bear to be alone in her own room... she would fall asleep on the couch and stay there all night. She came to the hospital only one or two more times in the whole five weeks that Caleb was at Harborview. It was very difficult for her to see her strong, capable brother reduced to the state he was in.

I still have a few upsetting memories of that week in the ICU. I clearly remember the first time the nurses had Caleb sitting in a chair. This was toward the end of that first week. I came in the morning, knowing that this was the day to get Caleb sitting up in a chair. In my naivety, I envisioned him sitting in a regular chair looking like a normal person. I was not prepared for what I was to see. I spoke to the nurse before I went into the ICU. He told me Caleb was in a chair. I specifically remember saying, "I'm so excited to see that." When I walked into the room I thought I might collapse... the chair was a massive contraption. I saw a black, padded, narrow bed that could be adjusted into a wheelchair apparatus. It was huge. To me, this was not a normal chair; it was grotesque. Caleb had one seatbelt around his chest and one around his legs. His body slumped and his head was limp. I had not expected the horror of a person in a vegetative state strapped to such a chair. This image terrified me. I imagined him being this way for the rest of his life... years of this vegetative, incapacitated state. When he was lying in a bed, he still looked "normal", but this chair was truly horrifying to me. I had to leave the room.

During that week I sobbed as I grieved his losses... even if he recovered... I could not image him being crippled. He was a phenomenal basketball player... he had potential for upper level college ball. Watching him play was like watching a gifted artist create. Basketball was so much a part of whom Caleb was... how could he be Caleb without basketball? I remember fighting sobs to tell my Mom, "Here he is lying in a coma, he may never wake up, and I am worried about whether or not he can play basketball! I feel so much guilt that this is important to me. I can't imagine him without basketball." Mom helped me through this... she reminded me that basketball was not just a sport for Caleb but part of his personality... of course it was hard for me to imagine Caleb without basketball. This week of facing the reality of a "different" Caleb was a week of severe agony. It is not even something I can adequately put into words. I prayed for recovery, but the reality was that even a strong recovery would mean the end of part of the Caleb I knew... this would be a new person... similar, but different... I felt that my son was gone and a new, unknown one would be replacing him.

Grieving

"My eyes are swollen with weeping, and I am but a shadow of my former self" Job 17:7 (NLT).

We think no one can know our grief... and to some extent that may be true. But others *can* know grief. Grief is not a contest. Because Caleb was healed, do I have less grief to bear than someone whose child dies? Because Caleb has new limitations cognitively and physically, do I have more grief to bear than someone who loses a dream? Grief is not meant to be stack ranked. The real question is "Can grief bond us to the Father?" I thought God could not really understand my grief of losing dreams and hopes for my child's future... He could not understand what it was like to lose the child I had nurtured. Caleb was still alive, but we had no contact, no relationship... he was lost to us... and we may never get him back. *But* gently He reminded me He does identify with my grief... not just because He is God and knows everything from some distant cerebral experience. Rather, in order for us to believe He can relate to us, He allowed Himself to *feel* and *experience* to the same depths that we feel and experience. The Father watched a precious Son face utter abandonment, humiliating rejection, inhumane beatings, absolute injustice, complete isolation, and agonizing death... DEATH. I looked death in the face, and my God had done the same.

Additionally, the Son experienced loss of the Father – complete separation. He was one with the Father and lost that. It was like cutting off a piece of Himself. When we feel that we will never be the same because a piece of our heart, a piece of who we are, is cut off and unredeemable, He has been there... He knows that kind of loss.

"Surely He has borne our grief and carried our sorrows"
(Isaiah 53:4 ESV).

While that means He carried the grief and sorrow *we deserved*, the verse means so much more. He carried the same *intensity* of grief and sorrow *we experience*. There is *no* depth we can go that He has not visited. That has double talk, so let me rephrase the point... Every depth we face has been visited by the Savior. Not only has it been visited by the Savior, but He has come out of it victorious... and so can we. He can carry us out of the depth because He knows the way out.... He IS the way out.

Chapter 3

Unfulfilled Expectations

CR

One week after the accident, Caleb was stable enough to move out of ICU and into the pediatric and burn victim ward. The same night Caleb was moved out of ICU, he opened his eyes for the first time. I thought this was a significant sign. Several friends were there and some knelt at the foot of the bed for over an hour waiting for Caleb to open his eyes again. I noticed Andy sitting in a chair away from the group. His face looked stressed. Later, I learned that the open eyes only pained him as he could not rejoice over this moment... it was still such an insignificant change.

As the next few days continued, we realized that even these early signs did not mean that Caleb would come out of the coma. The true definition of coma is somewhat difficult to pin down. Most definitions state that coma is marked by a person appearing to be asleep (eyes closed) and unable to be aroused by stimuli, including pain. Some medical professionals view a patient who remains completely unresponsive and who lacks any purposeful interaction with the environment as being comatose, regardless of the eyes being open or closed. Depending on the perspective of the health care professional, the open-eyed unresponsive state may be referred to either as a "coma" or as a "persistent vegetative state". Once eyes open, the brain does regulate a sleep cycle as such with open-eyed, unresponsive "awake" periods and close-eyed "asleep" periods. As we learned about these patterns of coma, the open eyes really gave no comfort since Caleb still showed no sign of awareness of stimuli or the environment around him.

The next stage we encountered was a season of "storming". Storming is caused by the brain signaling increased stimulation of the adrenalin glands leading to heightened stress response and neurological synaptic pathway firing. This storming was an agonizing time, and for over two weeks, Caleb stormed sixteen to eighteen hours every day. During the storming episodes, Caleb would thrash around the bed uncontrollably and sweat continually. His episodes lasted for forty-five to sixty minutes, stopped for a brief period of fifteen to thirty minutes, and began again in what seemed like a never ending cycle. This hyperactivity in addition to the brain's injured state caused Caleb to lose a considerable amount of muscle mass and overall body weight. In one week, he lost twelve pounds. By the time the storming subsided, he had lost around twenty-five pounds. His legs were bruised from hitting the rails of the bed, and he had open bed sores on his heals from rubbing against the sheets.

Many nights, Andy's Aunt Sally and I would sit on the bed; she would hold Caleb's legs and I would hold his body to keep him from injuring himself further. He would thrash and kick with great strength. I hated to leave at night because I knew that this would continue all night long. We had to strap restraints around wrists and ankles each night so that Caleb would have less chance of injuring himself while we were not in the room. It was disturbing to watch the storming, and many of Caleb's friends stood frozen with pained, fearful looks on their faces as they observed these storming episodes.

Even more distressing than this terrible storming was seeing Caleb's eyes as he stared off into the distance with a blank gaze. That gaze was one of the hardest things to take. The hollowness of his stare cut through me as if I was invisible. His eyes were wide open with enlarged pupils as he stared right at me. But those eyes showed no real life or spark; they were just an empty shell. People say the eyes are the window to the soul. Caleb's soul seemed so far buried that I felt he was in a distant place, alone and unreachable. Caleb often uttered moaning noises that sounded like alienated crying. The combination of the hollow stares and the crying sounds tore at my heart, and I felt that my child lay in an inaccessible existence of limbo. He wasn't really with us nor was he in heaven with the Lord. I had to trust that God would not leave him alone and frightened. My prayer became, "Lord Jesus, minister to him in this buried place. Let his spirit know that he is not isolated, but that You are there."

Because the storming was so unsettling, many people could only bear short visits. But for me, I had to be there as much as possible. I wanted to protect Caleb's body from self-inflicted wounds, but more than that, I wanted to talk with him and try to bring a soothing voice into his distant world. I tried to focus on the one positive of the storming... the signs of God's preservation. Caleb's storming caused the muscles to tense and flex for several hours each day, which prevented total muscle deterioration. Although he lost an alarming amount of weight (he went from 155 pounds to 130 pounds), his body had few bed sores other than those on his heels, and his muscles were stimulated and working.

After two or three weeks of storming, we still saw very little change in the coma status. Caleb was still deeply submerged. I was grateful to a friend who offered to go to Harborview and sit with Caleb on Sunday mornings so Andy and I could go to church; I needed that greatly. I've always had a personal connection to music, and the words of the worship songs ministered to me as did the sermons based on the first epistle of John. Many of the songs and messages touched me and reminded me of my need to trust God and to leave Caleb in His hands. While I wanted to do this, it was overwhelmingly painful. I feared that God would take Caleb... and I had other fears and guilt as well.

I don't remember the date, but it must have been after about a month at Harborview. After service, Pastor Walt offered opportunity for individuals to come up front for prayer as we were dismissed. Already fighting tears, both Andy and I went up. We sobbed as we collapsed onto the steps. Our pastor and two elders were with us. Walt asked us what our greatest pain was. Andy said, "Why isn't God healing Caleb? We have prayed and waited, but there doesn't seem to be any change."

I was afraid to share my pain... almost as if voicing it would confirm that I was right. But the pain was so severe that I could no longer keep it to myself. I finally voiced what I had been holding back, "I know I hold on too tightly to the kids. I have always felt that the one thing I could never bear is if something happened to one of the kids or Andy. Now it has happened to Caleb, and I'm afraid it's my fault. Maybe God let this happen to Caleb because I hang on too tightly. Maybe the accident is my fault!" I don't remember exactly what our pastor said, but he was compassionate and comforting. His words consoled me that... of course, a parent never wants something like this to happen. Any parent would feel that this is a pain more overwhelming than we can handle. God knows how much we love our children. He doesn't punish us for loving them so much. He wants us to trust Him, but He wasn't punishing us or letting this happen because I needed "a lesson". Praise God, this reminder helped me to release some of the crushing guilt I was carrying. Even today, I still have to fight the temptation to go back into feeling guilt over this... the Devil knows my vulnerability... but in my heart, I know that God is sovereign, He loves us, and He was not punishing us through this.

Yield

"Have mercy on me, O God, have mercy on me, for in you I take refuge. I will take refuge in the shadow of your wings until the disaster has passed" Psalm 57:1 (NIV).

Yield... give up... surrender... defer... What keeps us from yielding? In my life, the greatest barrier is fear. I can spend hours ruminating on ways to "solve" the situations I fear. Playing scenarios in my head, I "test" and evaluate solutions for the obstacles in my life. My behavior implies that if I find the "right" solution, I can avoid the danger that I fear. But I don't *really* hold that much control over my life. Surrender. What does that imply? That word implies that I am trapped. There is *no* other out. I am backed into a corner, and the *only* way to avoid destruction is to surrender. No one wants to get to that point in any situation. We resist losing control.

But something or someone will always have control. My option is to decide on and surrender to what will control me. I easily surrender to fear. That comes very naturally to me. I become paralyzed and ineffective. Fear takes me out of the game. It leaves me powerless and drops me in a heap cowering into a corner. I can surrender to guilt. Guilt often drives to action. Guilt suggests I can do something to rectify the situation. If I am good enough, strong enough, righteous enough, then I can change the situation. Or at least I could regain favor with God so *He* will change the situation. I can surrender to anger. I believe anger is really just an extension of fear. But where isolated fear is powerless, anger gives fear power and direction. Anger can be focused on someone. If no one else if available, it can be focused on God. Anger gives the illusion of power and that offers an illusion of regained control. Fear, guilt, and anger all seem to leave me with some type of control. If nothing else, I retain control of my reactions... and that makes me feel "powerful" over the situation.

But what if I surrender to the grace of Jesus? That is risky. I have to be willing to relinquish *all* control. I have to lay down fear, guilt, and anger. I have to release and surrender what I value... my sons, my daughter, my spouse, my finances, my health, my security. I need to come to a place where I can praise and bless the Lord *no matter what* I go through. This is why people who suffer love Job. In chapter 1, Job loses just about everything... his livestock, his wealth, and *all* his children. What does God leave him with? Job is left with his bitter wife who tells Job to "curse God and die" (Job 2:9). How supportive and helpful is that? Job grieved. He tore his clothes, shaved his head, and fell to the ground... but he worshipped!

"Naked I came from my mother's womb, and naked shall I return. The Lord gave, and the Lord has taken away; blessed be the name of the Lord" (Job 1:21 ESV).

Job surrendered to the grace of God. Job recognized that all good things come from God. Not only that, but Job recognized that our good God deserves to be praised and trusted, regardless of our circumstance. Job took refuge in God. I don't just surrender because I am trapped. I surrender because that is exactly the place I can find refuge. There is no refuge in my fear, guilt, or anger... but there *is* refuge in Jesus.

Chapter 4

Hurdles

℘

We now had the task of trying to find a facility for Caleb while waiting for a hopeful awakening. Harborview's job is saving lives, and they had done all they could do. From there, a transitional site was needed until Caleb would wake up and be ready for rehab at Seattle Children's Hospital. Finding a care facility proved to be a daunting task. We contacted several facilities, and most of them were not equipped to house a person in coma with such a severe brain injury. In addition, very few sites were willing to take a minor. We hit several walls.

So, we considered the idea of bringing Caleb home. When this idea first came to me, I felt that I was already taking on a large portion of Caleb's daily care at the hospital. I was also learning that even with so little known about why and how people recover from a coma, much research suggests that hearing the voices of familiar people can be a key to "waking up". I felt that we needed to find a solution to allow his friends easy access for visiting Caleb – any time of the day. After pondering these factors, I prayed about whether we should bring Caleb home. I was uncertain that Andy would feel comfortable with the idea because it would be *so* taxing on me. I knew Andy felt concerned about the stress level and the health implications for me. However, I felt that this was the best way to preserve my health. Caleb coming home took away my need to drive long distances to care for him. Furthermore, my presence at home would allow me to provide emotional support for Josh and Sarah. By taking on Caleb's care, I would remove the tension of feeling I could provide more consistent care than Caleb would receive in a facility. I prayed that Andy and I could come to a peaceful decision on this in which we would *both* feel it was the right move.

As I suggested the idea to Andy, I began to share my feelings on the benefits to Caleb and our family if Caleb came home. I didn't even have a chance to share all of the reasons I felt this was best before Andy stopped me and said, "If we can find a way to care for Caleb at home with no risk to him, then I am in favor of the idea." Again, I felt God had gone ahead of us... His confirmation that we were making the right choice came in the fact that Andy and I were unified in this decision to bring Caleb home. This situation could have become a huge tension point if we were not unified, but right from the very first voicing of the idea, we were in agreement on exploring this option.

Bringing Caleb home, of course, presented a whole new list of hurdles to jump. Where could we set up a make shift room for him? We were using our formal dining room/living room area as a recreation room, so we planned to modify that into Caleb's space. This gave us a place on the ground floor with good visibility from the kitchen and a large enough area to place a hospital bed and the necessary supplies. The room was open and bright and provided a space for me to care for Caleb while we both were in the hub of the home. We had a couch for nighttime caregivers to rest, and the room was large enough to have friends visit. We felt confident to move forward with the plan.

Another huge concern was how bringing Caleb home would impact Josh and Sarah. Josh was a senior in high school and had stayed very even throughout the roughest times thus far. He was accepting of the idea, but Sarah was very unsettled about bringing Caleb home. It was extremely difficult for her to see her brother in this helpless state. He had always been so lively, capable, and strong; she looked up to him. Now he was completely helpless and unresponsive. She had only been able to handle the hospital a couple of times during the past five weeks. She wasn't sure if she could be at peace with him home. How could she have a respite from the trauma we were facing as a family? We tried to encourage her and comfort her fears, but we knew this may be a difficult adjustment for her. Notwithstanding the hurdles, we felt that bringing Caleb home was the best solution for the situation. Unfortunately, this was the truth that our family had to face. Caleb may improve after coming home... or not... but we had to learn to come to terms with and live in the situation we faced as a family.

We began working with the social worker at Harborview to make this plan a reality. We needed to arrange for some in-home care givers. Caleb would benefit from a nurse and various therapists visiting periodically and routinely. As we explored our options, we discovered an organization named Rehab Without Walls. They provided in-home therapy and medical care for individuals recovering from various types of injuries – brain injury, stroke, spinal injury, etc. We hoped this might provide the perfect set-up for us. But, we had one large barrier.... Rehab Without Walls was not covered on our insurance. Maneuvering through the insurance maze, our truly remarkable social worker from Harborview wouldn't take 'no' for an answer. She worked with our insurance company and managed to get us good news. While Rehab Without Walls was not covered on our insurance, their parent organization was. The social worker informed us that insurance companies rarely cover groups outside the assigned companies, *but* they would make an exception in our case! Once again, God paved the path for this next step. Although we should not have gotten the approval at all since Rehab Without Walls was not formally on our list of covered care givers, our insurance agreed to fully cover Caleb's care through this program. Caleb would have all the rehab care we hoped for! This was a huge answer to prayer and the removal of a major barrier in bringing Caleb home.

Even with progress forward on the road to accomplishing our goal, we encountered one more huge wall to scale. Harborview informed us that we must have a doctor take on Caleb's case so that someone was responsible for his continued care while he was home. They suggested we have a neurologist, but most neurologists do not take on home-care cases. The next best thing would be a doctor specializing in internal medicine.

I knew our family doctor, Dr. Leou, had specialized in internal medicine, but would he be willing to take on the case? I called Dr. Leou one day while I was on my way to Harborview. He was a doctor we have always liked because he sincerely takes individual interest in his patients. He had a great memory and truly knew his patients. Dr. Leou had no idea of the accident or Caleb's serious situation, and he was saddened to hear the news. After hearing the details, Dr. Leou simply asked, "How can I help?" Well, I needed him to be willing to take our case and consult me over the phone for Caleb's care.

I don't know how many doctors would be willing to take on such a task... I would guess the list is quite short. But Dr. Leou didn't even hesitate; he was *very* open to taking on the case. I informed the staff at Harborview and asked them to update Dr. Leou as soon as possible. From that point, he took a role in setting wheels in motion to have the case transferred to his care. After seeing Caleb's file, Dr. Leou spoke with some of the neurology team at Harborview. He was quite concerned with the amount of Morphine that was routinely given to Caleb. The dose was high, and Dr. Leou insisted the Harborview team wean Caleb off half of the Morphine dosage before they released him.

Details began to fall into place. With a doctor taking the case and the rehab situation settled, we were able to arrange rental of medical equipment. We placed an order to rent a bed, lift, and wheelchair. We worked with a nutrition company to obtain the canned formula to feed Caleb through the G-tube (Gastrostomy tube – a feeding tube inserted through the abdomen directly into the stomach). The next hurdle presented itself: we must have a ramp into the house before Caleb could come home. I thought of the many friends who had told us, "Let us know how we can help." Gregg, a friend who worked construction, came to mind. I felt certain that he would have the skills to build a ramp for us. He came to visit us at the hospital one afternoon, and I asked him if he would be willing to construct a ramp up the few steps to the front door. I told him about our plan to bring Caleb home and that the doctors told us we needed a ramp in place. "I'll be there this weekend," was his response – and he was. Gregg and another friend, Doug, came over one evening, and within a couple of hours, the ramp was in place. Gregg even constructed a smaller, portable ramp to get from the sidewalk down one small step to the driveway. With these hurdles all crossed, the house was ready for Caleb to come home.

In preparation for Caleb's homecoming – and my need to care for him – I was required to spend forty-eight hours at the hospital to be trained in providing the complete care. The doctors were cautious about encouraging me to take on this task of home care. They were not really discouraging – they just took a very neutral stand. I'm sure they did not want to take on any liability in the case that my inexperience led to hurting Caleb further. Though I was determined to move forward, I craved some confirmation of my ability to meet the challenge. The Lord sent a few encouraging nurses. One nurse in particular, Trish, heard about our plan to bring Caleb home. She had seen the way I had cared for Caleb up to this point. She told me that some of the nurses had been discussing the plan and several of them had agreed; "If anyone can do this, you can," she told me. Many of the nurses were impressed that I was able to grasp Caleb's care needs and that I kept a cool head at the various situations that had arisen throughout the five weeks at Harborview. These nurses felt I was capable, and knowing that boosted my confidence.

During Caleb's last week at Harborview, I arrived one morning with the intent to stay and care for him over the next forty-eight hours. Over the course of those two days, I learned to bed-bathe him and change his bedding while he remained in the bed. To replace linens, bedding from one side was loosened and rolled up next to Caleb's body. Next, I would roll Caleb onto the bare mattress so that the bedding could be pulled out from under him. Then the same process was reversed as I recovered the bed. Thankfully, I quickly learned how to bathe him and change bedding. This was not too difficult. I was taught how to keep the G-tube clean and functioning and how to administer various drugs, liquid formula, and water. The storming had been calmed by a "cocktail" of drugs, and I learned to administer various dosages of drugs – Propanolol, Risperdal, Clonidine, Morphine, and Trazodone – to keep Caleb calm.

While I was training at Harborview, another small boy was brought in as Caleb's roommate. This boy was about six years old and had been in a serious boating accident. He had been in a coma for three days and was now awake. The boy was alert, although he still slept many hours of the day. I stayed with Caleb around the clock, and he was restless and storming throughout the night. I slept little and talked to him through much of the night hoping that he could somehow hear my voice and that it would calm him.

I had held up under great stress over the past four weeks, but that night was an almost unbearable low point. I told God, "This is so hard. I am happy for that other mother and her boy. He is out of the coma. But why do I have to have this boy in our room?! He is out of his coma after three days, and I am into day thirty-five with no end in sight for my boy. This is more than I can bear." But God, Abba Father, helped me get through the night – even through the tears. My heart was breaking, but where else could I go but to the Lord? I just kept praying, "Please Lord, let my son come out of this."

One other incident really deflated me... we had asked to speak with a doctor on the neurology team. It was rare that we actually spoke with a doctor; we often spoke with the physician assistant or residents but not the seasoned doctors. Andy and I waited all day to meet with a doctor, but they were often busy into the night with trauma situations. Finally, around 9:30 p.m. or so, Andy had to go home. I planned to stay a while longer in hopes that the doctor would still make it. Around 10:00 p.m., I was about to give up on seeing the doctor when he finally came in. This was a doctor we had not met before. I asked him several questions, but the main question we had was what to expect from here on out. So I asked him what to expect as far as signs of awakening and purposeful action. With no emotion, he responded, "Don't expect any change for at least six months." Feeling my body react to that statement, I fought the impulse to crumple to the floor. Six months! And no guarantee even after that. Such disheartening news crushed me. It was July and we were looking at this situation to last until Christmas or longer.

I know the medical staff did not want to give false hope, but this answer felt like *no* hope. As much as we were grateful for the care Caleb had received at Harborview, the place became very oppressive to me. It felt like a place of "no hope". We were now playing the waiting game. I really could not bear to go to Harborview anymore. The day before Caleb came home, I didn't even go in to Harborview; I had reached my saturation point of stamina in that place. All the hurdles had been crossed... it was time for Caleb to come home.

Hope

"My soul, wait in silence for God only, for my hope is from Him. He only is my rock and my salvation, my stronghold; I shall not be shaken. On God my salvation and my glory rest; the rock of my strength, my refuge is in God. Trust in Him at all times, O people; pour out your heart before Him; God is a refuge for us" Psalm 62:5-8 (NASB).

We use the word *hope* so casually today. "I hope I get a good grade... I hope I get to take that trip... I hope I get well... I hope _____..." I am struck by several variations of definition in *Merriam-Webster's Collegiate Dictionary*. Hope is defined as, "trust or reliance... a desire accompanied by expectation of or belief in fulfillment... someone or something on which hopes are centered."[1] Each of these insights pushes me further toward understanding the word *hope*.

"Trust or reliance" sounds like security to me. There is an assurance implied by those words. Often times, hope is not thought of as assurance but more as a dream or a wish. Dreams and wishes contain an element of "magic" which seems less than certain. But reliance does not wobble. It is firmly grounded. Hope that grows out of reliance is a sure thing.

"A desire accompanied by expectation of or belief in fulfillment" did speak to my state of mind at this point in Caleb's recovery. We were not given much hope from the healthcare staff. They did not have an expectation of or belief in his chances of waking out of the coma. Looking at the situation from a scientific perspective, we should not have had hope either. But my "desire accompanied by expectation and belief" settled deep...

1. By permission. From *Merriam-Webster's Collegiate® Dictionary, 11th Edition* ©2014 by Merriam-Webster, Inc. (www.Merriam-Webster.com)

and my expectations and beliefs rested in a supernatural power not a medical power. I felt defeated and hopeless many days. Perhaps out of naivety, or hopefully faith, I actually *did* expect Caleb to come out of the coma. So that was hope.

"Someone or something on which hopes are centered" swings the door wide open. *Someone* gave me hope. And my hope rested in that Someone – God. I had to trust in, rely on, expect of, and believe in that Someone and His fulfillment of a purpose in this tragedy. I *hoped* He would bring Caleb back to us. But what if He did not? Could I still be assured of His presence? Could I still trust Him? While I did hope for my desires to be fulfilled, I needed to focus on my needs, not desires, being met. I may not receive my desire – Caleb fully restored – but I could rely on and hope in being given the strength to endure the end result of the incident. Hope must go beyond whether or not my human expectations are met. Hope must stand firm regardless of outcome. In myself, I do not have nor can I hang onto hope. But hope is a gift. The Someone I hope in actually gives me the ability to hope. Regardless of outcome, I can be hopeful because of His assurance that He will stand with me.

So as I struggled through the fears and trials of my situation, my definition of hope developed and solidified. Hope is trust and reliance in Someone who is the center of my beliefs and expectations and who promises to fulfill my needs. If I can believe that He will stand with me regardless of circumstance, then I will be able to hold onto hope.

Chapter 5

Siblings

CR

I do not want to neglect the impact that summer had on our family as a whole... not only for Caleb... or for me... or for Andy. The impact of this trauma on Josh and Sarah should not be overlooked.

At seventeen, Joshua looked forward to his senior year of high school. He is an oldest son... and he takes that responsibility very seriously. While Caleb was at Harborview, Josh came often. Normally, he came with other friends, but he was steady and solid through every visit. He never showed much emotion, but he told me later that he always believed Caleb would recover from the injury. It was not a naïve expectation, but a real peace he had received from God. Josh took on all the responsibilities of senior year with very little help from me. He completed college entrance exams and applications. He stayed on top of all the senior activities and duties that are necessary for graduation. He never complained that I was out of touch with that part of his life. He just graciously took care of his own needs.

During the first week after the accident, Josh viewed an incident that gave him a confidence in Caleb's healing and recovery. Since we live in the foothills of the Cascade Mountains, it is common to see a variety of wildlife in our yard – elk, deer, black bear, raccoon, coyote. One morning, as Josh walked into the kitchen, he noticed two male deer walking through the yard. While deer are a normal sight for us, it is rare to see two bucks together. As Josh watched, he observed that one of the bucks was missing its left antler – Caleb had impacted on the left side of his face when he fell. The male deer with both antlers had two more points than the deer with a single antler – Josh is two years older than Caleb. Surprisingly, the male with two antlers patiently waited for the "damaged" male to follow along. Josh sensed that the presence of these two deer, each with specific physical qualities, was not by chance. He felt God was giving him an assurance that Caleb would recover from his injury but that he would need patient support. Josh felt a calling to be a brother who would patiently support Caleb to "come along" through his recovery. This event gave Josh a strong assurance and peace that God would heal Caleb. When I felt afraid and unsure of what we faced, Josh's peace never faltered. That peace bolstered me when I began to waver.

While several factors played into the man Josh has become, this event with Caleb strongly developed Josh's sense of responsibility for his family. He is gifted with a very protective nature. Throughout college and as he has stepped out into his career, he still holds onto a deep sense of being a support for the rest of us. He lives thousands of miles away from us, but when I talk with him on the phone, he still works to be that support. I can let my raw fears out with him, and he just says, "Mom, I am giving you a big hug from here, and I won't let go before we hang up." During his senior year, he felt led to study for military service. This was not because he is a person who glorifies war but because he feels such a strong calling to protect those who cannot protect themselves. Throughout college, God developed in him a profound will to stand in the gap for those who are victimized and mistreated by people who misuse power. I tend to believe that every event of his life – including the experience with Caleb's injury – drove him toward the desire to shield those who are marginalized and defenseless.

Thirteen is a rough year for any girl. But blend that with the type of trauma Sarah was experiencing, and that year can seem unbearable. From the start, Sarah was traumatized. She only came to the hospital a couple times during the five weeks at Harborview. Even then, she could only be in Caleb's room for a few minutes before she broke down. For those five weeks, I spent almost all day, every day, at the hospital. I am so grateful to friends who arranged a rotation of places for Sarah to stay. With wonderful foresight, one mom asked Sarah who *she* would be comfortable staying with. Then that mom made arrangements so Sarah had a place to stay every day and evening. Two families registered, paid for, and transported Sarah to basketball camp. I didn't even know she was going until they had it all arranged. For five weeks, Sarah was hardly home. That kept her occupied, but eventually, she had to face the reality of what was happening.

When we told Sarah that we would be bringing Caleb home from Harborview (still in a comatose state), she fell apart. She didn't think she could handle having the trauma in our home. With the reality "contained" at the hospital, she could avoid it, and home could be a sanctuary. But with Caleb, medical staff, and equipment coming into our home, her sanctuary would be lost. I felt trapped. Andy and I knew we could not put Caleb in a nursing facility; our best solution was to bring him home. But was it right to bring him home at the expense of Sarah? I understood her fear, but we are a family and this situation had to be faced together. I explained to her that whether we liked it or not, this was our "new normal" and we had to face the trial as a family... no matter what happened in the end. She did eventually feel a calmness about the situation. But a telling sign of her trauma was the fact that she could not sleep in her own room. From the day of the accident, Sarah's routine of sleeping on the couch in the living room lasted about five months before she could manage to sleep alone in her own room. We never pushed her on this. We just gave her the time she needed to adjust and to feel safe with being alone again.

I clearly remember one evening at dinner before Caleb came home. Sarah had plans to spend a day with a friend, but another friend invited her to a more appealing activity. Sarah wanted to change plans on the first friend and choose the more exciting option. Andy and

I tried to explain to her how hurtful it might be to the first friend, but Sarah would not let it drop. I finally lost it. I blew up at Sarah and "laid down the law" that she would not bail on the first friend. Blowing up in such a harsh manner was not my normal parenting style.

Instantly, I fell apart. I went up to my room and just wept. I had never been that biting with any of my children. The stress of the situation had pushed me to a reaction I did not know I was capable of. It shook me to my core. As I sat on my bed feeling like a complete failure as a mother, Josh came in. He calmly sat next to me and just put his arm around me. He told me Sarah knew I loved her and that she would be ok. Josh, the rock, again. Calm, rational, and comforting, he defused the situation.

A big part of our rationale for bringing Caleb home was so that I would be more available for Josh and Sarah... especially Sarah. With Caleb in nursing care, I would be away from home too often, with little end in sight. In spite of the questions we all had about how we could handle having Caleb at home, we felt it was necessary. Once Caleb came home, Josh and Sarah did remarkably well. Sarah watched often as the therapists worked with Caleb. She soaked in the methods and techniques that were used to stretch his muscles. Caleb experienced such severe spasticity in his right arm that his bicep was continually flexed and the arm would not straighten out. The therapists used massage and stretching in an effort to relax the muscle. But it was a slow process, and we gained little ground in regaining extension with the arm. In the evenings, Josh and Sarah would sit and gently stretch and massage the arm, just as they had observed the therapists do. Their patient treatment on Caleb's arm gave them a way to actively participate in Caleb's recovery. For Sarah, this was therapeutic.

After a few weeks of observing and participating in the treatments, Sarah began to voice an interest in pursuing a career in physical therapy. She held that dream for years but eventually modified that goal and studied nutritional dietetics. Though her interest morphed, she still sights the event of Caleb's accident and injury as the catalyst that prompted her interest in health care. Sarah suffered other consequences from that summer. As she matured, she faced many health issues that are at least partially related to the trauma her adrenal system suffered during a critical developmental stage. Through all the years of medical tests and specialists, God has shaped her into a compassionate woman who is well suited for a career in health care. I marvel at how God brought Sarah full circle. A trauma that could have emotionally shattered her was the very tool that God used to push her into a field where she will minister to others.

Father God

"But to all who did receive Him [Jesus], who believed in His name, He gave the right to become children of God, who were born, not of blood, nor of the will of the flesh, nor of the will of man, but of God" John 1:12-13 (ESV).

The experience that we all went through forced me to take a soul-searching look at who I really believe God to be. The term "god" can become a vague catch-all. Who is He really? I believe God to be a singular being of three distinct parts: Father, Son, and Spirit. That is a mindboggling concept no matter how I approach it. However, just as I have a mind, body, and soul that serve distinct purposes in my existence, the three parts of God serve unique and distinct roles. My purpose here is not to enlighten on how a triune God is possible, but to share how I grappled with my relationship to each of those roles of God.

I can easily relate to Jesus, the Son, who is my loving Savior. He loves me past all my failures, but even beyond that, He loves me enough to *pay* for all my failures and sin. He doesn't live in oblivion to who I am, but rather, He is keenly aware of who I am, loves me anyway, and takes my place of punishment. Then He gives me His Spirit to have the ability and strength to live a life more in line with His heart. I still fail, but I can know His Spirit still stands with me, forgives me, and puts me back on a right path. Jesus calls the Holy Spirit the Comforter, and I can feel secure that my relationship is "alright" with Jesus and His Spirit.

But Father is a powerful, holy judge. He feels imposing and unapproachable. I had to wrestle with the questions, "Is God punishing me? Is God punishing Caleb? Have I been too proud so that God has to teach and humble me at Caleb's expense? Do I put too much value in my children, and now God is taking one of them?" I did not want to face these questions, but yet, they nagged in the back of my mind. I knew then, and still know now, that I could never atone enough to be free from deserving Father God's punishment. Even when I *want* to live a "morally right" life, I blow it *every* day. How can I approach Someone who has every right to squash me? How can I feel safe to go to Father God?

Although I still struggle with how I envision Father God, I acquired new eyes to see Father God as my Papa or Daddy. I realize that for many people in the world, the term *father* conjures up disturbing, negative images. Tragically, too many fathers fail to fulfill that role as they may abuse or desert that position. But a man who genuinely represents all that is right and good about *father* uses strength and tenderness to protect and provide for his children. And any man who rightly reflects that image of father is only a faint representation of the perfect Father.

At first consideration, strength and tenderness may seem to contradict each other, but they actually complement each other. I recently read a passage from the prophet Isaiah which skillfully unites God's might and love,

"Behold the Lord God comes with might, and His arm rules for Him... He will tend His flock like a shepherd; He will gather the lambs in His arms; He will carry them in His bosom, and gently lead those that are with young" (Isaiah 40:10-11 ESV).

Powerful and tender. In Father God, they are *perfectly* united.

First of all, He comes with might. Mighty God holds the whole of creation in His hand. That image astounds me. His power is so vast that He could destroy me, or all of creation, with a thought. His power overshadows every power I could image. Isaiah expands chapter 40 with a few descriptive details to give us some perspective.

"Who has measured the waters in the hollow of His hand and marked off the heavens with a span, enclosed the dust of the earth in a measure and weighed the mountains in scales and the hills in a balance?" (Isaiah 40:12 ESV).

It almost feels like overkill as this one verse sparks from one image to the next. Do we really grasp the visual? Nearly 70% of the surface of our earth is covered with water. It is estimated that if we measured all of Earth's water (oceans, icecaps, lakes, rivers, groundwater, and atmosphere) there would be about 332,500,000 cubic miles of water. A cubic mile of water equals more than 1.1 trillion gallons of water. I will do the math for you... that is roughly 365 trillion gallons of water... held "in the hollow of His hand"! Scientists estimate the Milky Way galaxy to be about 100,000 light years in diameter. (*One* light year is a distance of about 9.5×10^{15} meters, which means the Milky Way diameter of 100,000 light years measures roughly 9.5 trillion billion meters across.) That is only the Milky Way, a mere fraction of the universe. Yet Isaiah says that God "marks off the heavens with a span". I cannot wrap my head around these vast figures... but seriously... God is powerful! That much power could be alarming and paralyzing to my soul. I am compelled to cower in the presence of such a terrifying Being. But wait. Isaiah does not stop with might. The next image presents a stark contrast to the might and power.

Going deeper, Isaiah reminds us that God gathers His children to His bosom. I am not sure we can imagine a more tender and protective scene than a father or mother snuggling a small child to his or her chest. Picture that act. Surrounding the child with strong arms, a parent shields the helpless being and bends to cover the fragile head of the child. Such an act exudes limitless love and protection. I see myself as that child. An ever attentive shepherd, Father God scoops me up from danger. He wraps me in arms bigger than the universe. He shields me from danger, enemies, and evil. No, I do not cower from the might of Father God, I run to it! When that might is paired with His immeasurable love, His might becomes a stronghold and refuge for me. Living outside His love would make His might a terrifying thing. It should be terrifying. His might is bigger than the universe. But living *within* His love (also bigger than the universe) transforms His might into a safe haven of power that *no* force can overcome.

As I began to grasp more of God's might woven through His love, I began to feel safer to draw near to Him. That new safety led to another reality about how Father God deals with me. Jesus refers to Father God with the Hebrew term "Abba". The implications for Abba Father God go deep. Abba is a covenant God. Covenant is an odd term. So what does it mean? Covenant is a formal and legally binding declaration. It is similar to a contract but so much more. A contract requires agreement and promise from both parties. If either party breaks the terms of the contract, the agreement is nullified, and the offended party is no longer bound by the promise. Covenant comes with promise from only one party; it is similar to a last will and testament. I do not do or promise anything to be included in the will of my parents; they include me out of their own desire to bless me. Abba offers covenant to me saying that He will love me. I accept this gift, but I have done nothing to earn or deserve the gift. He loved me even when I did not love Him. He loves me still even when I mess up. Because the covenant depends solely on Him and not on me, He could not love me any more *and* He could not love me any less. So Abba implies covenant. But the covenant Abba offers is not just a legally binding arrangement. His covenant is personal and intimate. He desires personal relationship with me... just as a truly loving father desires personal relationship with his child.

I know people who feel offended at a personal image of God as a Father who welcomes me to climb up on His lap. They feel the only respectful way to approach Father God is with "fear and trembling". That feeling of offense saddens me. The Bible is full of images of God gathering His children and lovingly shielding them. Yes, He is to be deeply respected. But I don't believe that He intends for us to feel afraid to approach Him. If a child is truly *afraid* to approach an earthly father, people suspect that the father has abused his power over the child. Abba Father is not abusive; He is tender and loving while still being mighty and powerful to save and protect. I can fully respect His authority and power while still feeling safe to run into His loving arms.

As I have wrestled with all these truths about God, I have gained confidence to approach Him. He used to seem imposing and unapproachable. Now I see him as welcoming and approachable. His power used to seem harsh and terrifying. Now I know it is gentle and comforting. In the light of His love for me as His child, Abba Father shows me two qualities of His character: He is mighty enough to shield and protect me, and He loves me enough to do so.

Chapter 6

The New Normal

CR

Wednesday, July 26, 2005 – The day Caleb came home. I went to the hospital in the morning. There were some final details to arrange. Caleb still had pins securing a fracture in his arm, and those pins had to be removed. I needed to pick up ten medications from the pharmacy and arrange the final ambulance transport. One by one, details were checked off and check-out paperwork was completed. The ambulance was scheduled to pick up Caleb around 3:00 p.m. I headed home to set up and to be ready for Caleb's arrival. Caleb arrived home and our Rehab Without Walls nurse dropped by around 6:00 p.m. to check on various needs and answer questions. Relief washed over me as we finally had Caleb home – no more trips to Harborview. Lately, I had come to a point where I dreaded going to Harborview, which conflicted with the unbearable thought of leaving Caleb alone there. Now, a more peaceful feeling came over me as we finally had our son home again...

Caleb was home, but we were far from the end of this ordeal. Caleb's schedule required administration of nutrition and medication every four hours around the clock, so we placed a couch beside his bed for night time caregivers. Andy contacted and organized about thirty people to join my "helper team". These people took various shifts during the day or night to give me a break. We particularly wanted helpers at night so I could sleep at least six good hours in order to be functional during the day. I trained each helper to become comfortable with G-tube feedings, measuring and administering medications, and changing clothing and bedding. But until I could sufficiently train the team, I took both day and night shifts.

The first Wednesday night and Thursday went well. But Thursday night brought a new concern as Caleb developed a fever. During the night, I checked his fever every hour. I administered liquid Tylenol through the G-tube and used cool cloths to try to keep his temperature down. But even though the temperature went down for a short time, it held in at about 103^{0}F throughout the night. By about 4:00 a.m., I was getting really worried. I knew extended fevers can cause brain damage for even healthy individuals... and we were already facing permanent brain tissue damage from the accident. Panic surged through my body as I feared additional brain damage from the fever. I called the emergency service for Dr. Leou, but another doctor from his office was on call. She had little knowledge of Caleb's situation, but said that we should call an ambulance if I could not keep the fever down.

By 5:00 a.m. I could not wait any longer. Andy was asleep in our room, and I went up to tell him what was happening. I woke him and told him that I could not keep the fever down. I felt like a limp rag-doll. I just collapsed on the bed. I didn't even have the energy to cry. I just whimpered in weak sighs. I remember thinking, "What am I doing? How can we possibly take care of Caleb? I don't have the medical knowledge to deal with these serious issues. We may have made a big mistake." Andy also felt overwhelmed. He told me later that this was the moment when he truly feared we would lose Caleb. After all we had gone through, it seemed like Caleb would not make it after all.

We decided to call 911. Andy was scheduled to take tests in his training classes that morning. I would go with Caleb to Overlake Hospital, but we felt I should not go alone. We called a friend, Warren, and asked if he might be able to go with me. Thankfully, Warren was able to accompany me, and he got to our house before the emergency vehicles arrived.

A fire truck and ambulance responded to the 911 call. Two of the EMTs remembered Caleb since they had been at the scene of the original accident. In all my uncertainty, I still felt unsure if calling them had been overreacting, but they were very kind and assured us that it was right to call them. They took vitals and asked questions, and then the ambulance workers loaded Caleb into the ambulance. I was to ride with Caleb, and Warren would follow in his car. I quickly grabbed a bag with medications, feeding syringe, formula, extra diapers and clothes. I really had no idea how long we would be gone... or if Caleb would even be able to come back home with me.

At Overlake Hospital, the doctors ran some tests and took chest x-rays. Nothing conclusive was found after the tests. The doctors felt it may just be a virus that Caleb was fighting. After about four hours, Caleb was again loaded into the ambulance for the ride home. I rode home with Warren. We continued to treat the fever for a full week after the visit to Overlake Hospital, but we were hopeful that it was not too serious. Finally, by the following Thursday, we managed to get through an entire night with his temperature staying below 100°F.

His fever lingered sporadically for several weeks. Although we were past the worst of it, Caleb's temperature still shot up and down. During this time, Caleb began experiencing restless periods, and he would sweat often, even with fans and an AC unit near his bed. Unfortunately, since he was still completely unconscious, there was no way to know what was happening in his body. Later, we realized Caleb was actually fighting narcotic withdrawal symptoms.

From the moment he took the case, Dr. Leou was concerned about the high doses and large number of medications administered to Caleb. Even before Caleb came home from Harborview, Dr. Leou had required the hospital staff to cut Caleb's morphine dosage in half. Once Caleb got home, Dr. Leou and I decided to slowly wean Caleb off one drug at a time. Dr. Leou felt, "How can we know if he *could* wake up? The high doses of medications may be preventing him from coming around." Tapering off the prescribed drugs was a risky task because the combination of medications was supposed to keep Caleb balanced to prevent violent storming, seizures, or restlessness; however, we felt systematically weaning Caleb was worth the chance. Morphine was the first drug to go, and we cut the remaining morphine doses cold turkey. As time went on, Caleb continued to show consistent restlessness, ongoing sweating episodes, and random temperature swings. More and more we began to believe that Caleb was experiencing morphine withdrawal.

In the end, his unconscious state through the withdrawal stage was really a blessing. To this day, he remembers none of the terrible side effects he experienced during this difficult morphine withdrawal period. As I witnessed the physical reactions, I fought concern that this may be too much for his body, but once we had eliminated the drug, Dr. Leou felt we should stay the course. After a couple weeks of restlessness, Caleb finally began to move past the harsh symptoms. We had eliminated the strongest drug from his "cocktail" of medications, and we experienced no adverse reactions or recurring storming. This was a good sign, and we were encouraged to continue the weaning process.

Dr. Leou was truly a vital asset to my ability to care for Caleb. From the start, he told me to call any time... and I did... often. I spoke with him several times each week. I kept close records of Caleb's vital signs (pulse, blood pressure, and temperature) and reported to Dr. Leou regularly. Any time a serious concern arose, I called. Since he had other patients to care for, I normally left a message, and he would have to return my calls. But, he always called back... often times after 6:00 p.m. when he had finished his day of seeing patients. We would consult for twenty to thirty minutes and decide together on the next step. He valued my input, as I was the one in daily contact with Caleb, and he directly encouraged me that I was "doing a good job". His trust in me gave me confidence that I was making good decisions and giving effective care. He guided me through weaning Caleb off all the medications, and he took steps to move Caleb toward awakening, not just maintaining status quo. He routinely evaluated our situation, advanced our plan toward recovery, and counseled me over the phone. I know he felt he was just doing what any caring doctor would do, but we felt he went *way* beyond what many doctors would do under such unusual circumstances.

Once we had completely weaned Caleb off morphine, we began to taper off the other drugs. Slowly, I eliminated the Propanolol, Risperdal, Clonidine (three medications used to regulate blood pressure and agitation). Less than a month after Caleb's homecoming, we had eliminated all the drugs except for a light dose of Trazodone to help with night sleeping cycles. Throughout the weaning process, Caleb never regressed back into storming stages, and he never suffered any seizures. He continued to exhibit an unresponsive comatose state, but at least we could evaluate whether lack of responsiveness was due to his brain injury or to the drug-induced suppression of brain activity.

In addition to weaning off the medications, Caleb received intensive therapy through Rehab Without Walls. The speech therapist first began by simply teaching me methods to keep Caleb's mouth clean. While at Harborview, he had acquired a severe yeast infection in his mouth, so I literally brushed and scraped his tongue with a liquid medicine to combat the infection. Any time we used a liquid in his mouth, I used a suction device to draw the fluids out to prevent the possibility of choking. He was incapable of swallowing at this point, so we took extra precautions to make sure all liquids were removed. I learned how to brush his teeth using the suction device and wedging a tongue depressor between his teeth so that he could not lock his jaw on the toothbrush. Once while the therapist and I were cleaning his mouth with a sponge tool, Caleb bit down and pulled the small sponge off of the stick and into his mouth. I knew this could pose a serious choking threat, so I shoved my finger between his teeth and forced his jaw open so that the therapist could retrieve the sponge. My fingers showed bite marks from the pressure of Caleb's reaction to bite down, but we got the sponge out quickly. The therapist and I both took deep breaths as our hearts pounded at the thought of how serious this could have been.

The speech therapist also took on the task of trying to reach Caleb mentally. We needed to prompt a conscious response. In an early visit, she asked me about his interests. I shared who he was as a basketball player and how much that skill had shaped his goals and dreams. She wanted to use familiarity to reach him and suggested we use a basketball to prompt him toward consciously grasping at an object. This was very painful for me. I asked her if there was any possibility he would ever play basketball again. She said that his injury was very severe and that he would probably never play again. This stabbed me like a knife. I knew his injury was severe, and I wanted to be grateful for any steps toward having Caleb back. But basketball was more than a game to Caleb. It was a defining quality of who he was. I said to her, "I understand he may lose basketball, and if that is so, isn't it cruel to use a basketball to coax him?" She responded that we would use *anything* we could to reach him. He was so far under that coma that we needed every tool available to us. After we broke through, then we could decide if we should continue using something related to basketball. But, we had to break through, and any method available to us needed to be fair game.

We also had an occupational therapist. His job at first was to stretch Caleb's upper body in order to maintain flexibility and range of motion. Caleb's severe muscle spasticity in his right arm caused his bicep to form a large knot, and the arm was incapable of being straightened. This could eventually become a serious problem. The brain was sending a signal for the muscle to flex continually, and over time, this may become irreversible. Our daughter Sarah was a trouper. She would massage Caleb's arm each night and attempt to loosen the muscle. We considered casts or braces to force the arm to straighten, but as time went on, the arm began to loosen up. Again, there was no good medical explanation for this healing. Caleb's arm should not have relaxed without some type of significant treatment... but it did.

The physical therapist worked Caleb's lower body. Again we used many stretching exercises to prevent permanent tightening of muscles. We tried to sit Caleb up at times to familiarize his system to an upright position since the body loses equilibrium after lying flat for so long. In early August, we could get him to sit (assisted) for about one to two minutes and stand (assisted) for about thirty seconds. The standing goal was to put weight on his bones because bones begin to weaken and become brittle without routine weight bearing to strengthen the bone tissue. Since he still showed only reflex-type interaction with his surroundings, he needed support from two people, but we managed to get him up to sitting and standing positions for very short sessions several times a day.

In addition to the therapist, an assistant came two to three times a week to continue the stretching routines. For the first two weeks, there was really little change in the status. It was a heavy time of training for me. We usually spent three to four hours a day with some type of therapist.

With my new "normal", I got up each morning and showered to meet my day. Then I spent thirty minutes every morning bathing Caleb and changing bedding. Now, this all had to be done with him in the bed. I had special rinse-free soap and shampoo, and I gave him a full bed bath each morning. Next, I changed his bedding under him by using the process I had learned at Harborview. Once he was bathed and positioned on new bedding, I could dress Caleb in clean clothes. The final task of the morning routine was to administer his G-tube feeding before his therapists began to arrive. Depending on the day, we would have two to four hours of therapist visits. When Caleb and I were alone after therapy sessions, I carefully worked through additional stretching exercises to help keep his muscles loose. These routines consistently filled my days.

After about three weeks at home, we hit a plateau. There was still no conscience response. Caleb had open eyes, but there was no visible recognition of anything happening around him. They were still hollow eyes. It still seemed that no one was behind the stare. Again I prayed, "Lord, where is he? He is not with us and he is not with You... he is alone. Be with him in his aloneness. Speak to his spirit and let him know that You are with him, even in this lost place." Even after weeks of working to reach him, the haunting stares gave heart-piercing reminders of his comatose state.

As we stalled out on a plateau, the rehab team was forced to make adjustments to Caleb's therapy routine. The occupational therapist and physical therapist could still do stretching and muscle training, but it was difficult to justify two or more visits a week from the speech therapist. Her next job should be to help Caleb learn to talk, swallow, and eat again. Since he was still completely unresponsive, we were required to move to one visit a week for speech therapy. This represented a disappointing step backward, but it seemed unnecessary to have her move forward while Caleb was still unresponsive.

Then we saw the first significant step forward...

Not Alone

"He said, 'Go forth and stand on the mountain before the Lord.' And behold, the Lord was passing by! And a great and strong wind was rending the mountains and breaking in pieces the rocks before the Lord; but the Lord was not in the wind. And after the wind an earthquake, but the Lord was not in the earthquake. After the earthquake a fire, but the Lord was not in the fire; and after the fire a sound of a gentle blowing" 1 Kings 19:11-12 (NASB).

I felt a strong sense of faith in God before Caleb's accident. Some people would call me a "cradle Christian" because I cannot remember a time when I did not know Jesus loved me and saved me. But Caleb's accident and months of recovery stretched that faith more taut than I had ever experienced. As weeks and months of a comatose state continued, I felt completely spent. It felt risky to hope. I faced a feeling of isolation like I have felt no other time in my life. So often, people who suffer are faced with the question, "Can anyone *really* understand how I feel?" Suffering can become so intense that it seems unlikely that anyone, even God, could possibly grasp the depth of our personal despair. I hit that low spot one night.

My strength waned and progress seemed so unlikely that I landed in a pit of grief and despair. In my complete hopelessness, I called out to the Lord, "Lord, how can you know how I feel? You don't know what it is like to lose a son." Now, I would not say I have ever heard an audible voice from God, but in that moment, my spirit definitely "heard" the Lord speak to me. There was no rock rending wind, ground shattering earthquake, or consuming fire, but I perceived a gentle blowing sound. God answered me in my despair. "Yes, I do. I *do* know what it is like to watch a Son suffer and die."

That was all. No profound or prophetic word. Just a simple reminder of the suffering the *Father* experienced as He watched His Son endure torment, humiliation, and death. I stood dead in my tracks at the sudden grasp that God had "walked in my shoes". He *did* understand. My circumstance had not changed. Caleb still lay comatose with no certain sign of a change happening any time soon. But I received a more keen awareness and understanding of this truth:

"No temptation has overtaken you but such as is common to man; and God is faithful, who will not allow you to be tempted beyond what you are able, but with the temptation will provide the way of escape also, so that you will be able to endure it" (1Corinthians 10:13 NASB).

That moment, brief as it was, remains seared in my mind. In that instant, I received a new intimacy with Father God. I realized that He moved beyond seeing my grief... He chose to *share* my grief. Why would He choose that? He so deeply desires intimacy with me that He descends to where I am. This descent goes so far beyond the fact that He took human form and came to Earth to live. Even though Jesus descended to provide a way of escape from my ultimate death, in *this* life I still struggle. Incapable of ascending to Him, I remain here in my mortal, lowly state of weakness. But remarkably, He never leaves me alone in that crushed state... He descends to be my companion in that low place.

"The Lord is near to the brokenhearted and saves the crushed in spirit" (Psalm 34:18 ESV).

Hear what that verse says. In my brokenhearted and absolutely crushed state, He comes to me!

That is what I experienced in His quiet voice speaking to my spirit. "I *know*... I know the depth of your despair. I know the loss you feel. I know the isolation you feel. I know... And because I know how completely alone you feel, I will not leave you alone. I will stay near."

Chapter 7

Breakthrough

CR

On Sunday, August 21, a long-time friend, Peter, sat with Josh as the boys visited in Caleb's room. I was in the kitchen when Peter called to me, "Kim, Caleb just took a hat out of my hand." I was really unaffected by this. Caleb had made subconscious movements and responses to the environment around him, but it was still underneath the comatose state. But I always tried to keep a positive outlook when Caleb's friends were over, so I went to watch. As I stood there, I could not believe my eyes! Caleb took the hat from Peter several times. It was not a subconscious, automatic response; it was a very intentional action. Caleb looked at the hat, reached for it, and repeated the action. This was his first purposeful response! Fear from past disappointments made it difficult to be too excited, but this was an incredibly hopeful sign.

On Monday, the occupational therapist was scheduled to visit in the morning. He came at his normal time, and I told him about the way Caleb had grabbed the hat several times the evening before. I also mentioned that we could not tell if Caleb was really aware of us or if it was just a reaction to the environment. "Let's find out," was the occupational therapist's response.

The occupational therapist took three balls of various colors. He held the balls in front of Caleb. "Caleb, can you take the pink ball?" he asked. Caleb responded correctly. Was it a fluke? "Caleb, can you take the orange ball?" he prompted again. Caleb responded correctly again. After several minutes of testing, the occupational therapist felt confident that Caleb knew what he was doing *and* that he was able to hear us and process the information. This was huge! Several health care providers had prepared us that even if Caleb woke up, he may not understand spoken language. The fact that he was able to understand, process, and react to verbal command represented progress more significant than anything so far experienced. We showed Caleb a family picture and had him point to Mom, Dad, Josh, and Sarah. He could identify each. Our occupational therapist had always been very reserved in his reactions to any changes, but I could see that even he was excited about this development. He knew that the new therapy plan scheduled our speech therapist to come only once a week since Caleb had been so unresponsive. The occupational therapist got on the phone with the speech therapist and told her the news. We would need her to come more often after all.

Now the *real* work began. Caleb would have to relearn *everything*... how to walk, swallow, eat, talk, use the bathroom... the list seemed daunting. A long road was still ahead of us.

Rehab now became very intense... and very difficult. Caleb was showing purposeful responses, but much of his awareness was still underneath a "haze". *Every* movement took great effort. If he had to reach for an object, it could take him several seconds just to raise his arm and move toward the object. Every instruction required patient waiting for Caleb to react.

The physical therapist took on the job of getting Caleb to sit up, stand, and hopefully, begin walking. During this grueling process, I was reminded of how easily we take for granted the routine physical acts we perform each day. The therapists spent time teaching Caleb how to grab a bed rail just to roll himself to the edge of the bed so he could learn to sit up on his own. I felt dumbstruck at how much effort it took for Caleb to perform a simple task that would require no thought or conscious effort for me. At first, Caleb resisted sitting or standing at all. Every time he moved into an upright position he became dizzy and nauseated which hindered him from standing for even thirty seconds at a time. In addition to nausea and dizziness, two months in a bed posed the hurdle of muscle atrophy, and his legs were so weak and unresponsive that it took two people to support him every time we stood him up. In spite of his struggles, we forced Caleb to push through these exercises since daily weight bearing was critical to preventing his leg bones from becoming brittle. This seemingly simple act of standing up required such exertion that Caleb became exhausted after a short session.

The occupational therapist spent time teaching Caleb to put on his own T-shirt. Again, this task required enormous effort, especially for his right arm which had so much spasticity. Caleb became frustrated and often wanted to give up. My self-control was tested as I watched him struggle time and time again, but I could not help him... he had to learn to cope on his own.

The speech therapist set many goals for Caleb. First, we just wanted to find a way to communicate with him. Since Caleb exhibited no ability to vocalize yet, our therapist used picture cards with the words 'yes' and 'no' for Caleb to point out answers. We had to be patient for his mental processing and slow physical response, but he could generally point to the correct card when prompted. Soon, he progressed to head nodding his answers. At first, he barely shook his head for 'no' but could not manage to nod for 'yes'. Because his movements were so small, I had to watch closely to discern whether he was actually responding. When I asked him a question and he did not respond, I assumed that was 'yes', and then I double-checked my assumption by inverting the sentence so he could answer with his 'no' head movements. Though simplistic, this system helped me reestablish communication with Caleb.

The speech therapist also had the task of teaching Caleb to swallow again. The first step was to observe a gag reflex. As I brushed Caleb's teeth each day, I waited for him to gag. It had never occurred to me that Caleb's brain would have to relearn reflexes. Even an infant can gag and swallow, but Caleb's brain had to relearn all these skills. Eventually, his gag reflexes responded. Next, she fed Caleb small ice chips to see if he had a swallowing reflex. He did well. He loved it when he could progress to small pieces of Popsicle. Needless to say, we kept a large supply of Popsicles in the freezer that summer!

As tough as it was, we intentionally pushed Caleb to develop a tolerance for sitting up. The therapy expectations were to progress to sitting up at least thirty minutes a day, and we sat him in a wheelchair several times a day to reach that goal. Many times he would seem unhappy with this. Sometimes he became frustrated and wanted back in the bed. Watching body language offered the only way to interpret his feelings and reactions. He really could not communicate well, so I monitored his stress level through his facial expressions. Often times I had to make the call to keep him in the chair until the agitation level seemed high enough to warrant moving him back into the bed.

Only three days after Caleb's first purposeful movement, several friends were over visiting and cleaning our house. Our therapy assistant and I transferred Caleb to his wheelchair. This process required us sitting next to him on the bed, supporting him on either side, and then standing him up. Next we tried to get him to pivot on one foot so that he could sit back into the chair. We got Caleb situated and wheeled him out onto the back porch to watch his friends. He often became highly agitated when we took him outside. I believe the sensory input (light, wind, sounds, open space) was too overwhelming, so he usually lasted only a few short minutes outside before he became distressed. On this day, he lasted over thirty minutes just watching his friends. Appreciating the moment, we celebrated a big step of forward progress.

As Caleb became more aware, he also became more frustrated. On the up side, awareness meant he could actively participate in his range-of-motion therapy. But on the down side, if he was hurting, confused, or frustrated, he could be difficult to work with. Sometimes he would swing at (a *very* slow, purposeful swing) or pinch people. He did seem to respond positively to me, and he would comply when I asked him to be gentle or to calm down. His behavior to settle down also encouraged us because it indicated that he knew who I was, could interpret my words, and could perform accordingly. That ability to decode, interpret, and respond to my verbal commands told us that the verbal speech center of his brain was still functioning. Considering the prognosis that Caleb may not be able to understand our speech, these reactions gave tremendous hope.

September 2 marked more significant improvements. The speech therapist felt Caleb was ready to try swallowing something more substantial than liquid. Dabbing tiny portions of pudding onto Caleb's lips, she coaxed him to lick it off with his tongue. Though he responded very slowly and deliberately, he managed to lick off the pudding and swallow! This thrilled Caleb as he had not tasted food for months. He *loved* any flavor we put into his mouth. This same day, Caleb took several steps. With support on both sides, he walked about eight steps from a couch to a chair. He made this trip about eight times with a short sitting break at each end. This represented truly remarkable progress. Although Caleb needed our support for balance, he had carried his own weight. We knew that Caleb may be wheelchair bound for much of his life. We even had an appointment for a personally fitted wheelchair. But these first steps brought encouragement that he may be able to reacquire some abilities to walk. In an effort to work fine motor skills, Caleb held crayons and labored to trace large letters. He struggled just to scribble a faint line. Though I painfully watched all these labored efforts, we felt greatly encouraged by each of these accomplishments.

Joy

"But let all who take refuge in You rejoice; let them ever sing for joy, and spread Your protection over them, that those who love Your name may exult in You" Psalm 5:11 (ESV).

"Joy is not the absence of suffering but the presence of God" (Anonymous). I saw this saying on a greeting card or wall plaque when I was a child. But the older I get, the more significant this quotation becomes to me. However, let's be honest, this quotation would not be the first thought that comes to mind for many of us. I think *Merriam-Webster's Collegiate Dictionary* definition fairly represents the way many people look at joy: "The emotion evoked by well-being, success, or good fortune or by prospect of possessing what one desires."[1] Yikes! This definition is hard to live up to. Well-being, success, good fortune, and getting what I want. What if life is not well, a failure, unfortunate, and not what I want? Is joy lost to me?

My personal life is not best expressed as a path of comfort, notable accomplishment, or opportune circumstances. I can cite a plethora of failures, losses, and struggles. My experience through Caleb's accident and recovery is only one event, albeit a significantly life impacting event, that brought challenges to my life path. If joy depends upon how "triumphant" my life is, then I must succumb to the reality that joy will pass me by. I must admit, I do not easily submit to a defeatist attitude. So, I am not willing to agree with Merriam-Webster on this definition. I feel much too limited by that definition... there must be more.

1. By permission. From *Merriam-Webster's Collegiate® Dictionary, 11th Edition* ©2014 by Merriam-Webster, Inc. (www.Merriam-Webster.com)

In my searching for a *joy* definition I could relate to, I found an interesting example in the book of Habakkuk. Habakkuk lived in a difficult – I could say highly *unsuccessful* – time. The nation of Israel was in bad shape spiritually and politically, and Habakkuk cried out to God for deliverance. But God's answer presented a surprise. Rather than tell Habakkuk, "Never fear! Success is on the way!" God answered by saying, in effect, "I am working on a plan that will astound you. I am going to raise up the Chaldeans. Yes, they are bitter, hostile, violent, downright nasty people, but I am putting them into power." Now at the time of Habakkuk, the Chaldeans were an insignificant nation. But the Chaldeans would later be known as the Babylonians. Most students of ancient history will note that the Babylonians became a very powerful nation. They conquered several nations, and they did not mind getting blood on their hands to do so. They became so powerful that they completely overran the people of Israel – Habakkuk's people – and carried the nation of Israel off into exile. This answer from God would *not* seem to encourage an attitude of joy. But wait... look at what Habakkuk says in chapter 3.

"I hear, and my body trembles; my lips quiver at the sound; rottenness enters my bones; my legs tremble beneath me. Yet I will quietly wait for the day of trouble to come upon people who invade us. Though the fig tree should not blossom, nor fruit be on the vines, the produce of the olive fail and the fields yield no food, the flock be cut off from the fold and there be no herd in the stalls..." (Habakkuk 3:16-17 ESV).

Habakkuk's situation sounds pretty hopeless... hard to hear any reason for joy in this listing of personal and national collapse... but wait for it...

"Yet I will rejoice in the Lord; I will take joy in the God of my salvation" (Habakkuk 3:18 ESV).

Joy! Joy because no matter how bad it gets, God offers me salvation. No failure, no enemy, no conqueror – no accident, no physical disability, no loss – can take that salvation from me. Now *that* is reason for joy. And there is more...

"God, the Lord, is my strength; He makes my feet like the deer's; He makes me tread on my high places" (Habakkuk 3:19 ESV).

Not only does He *give* me salvation and joy in time of loss and struggle... He *is* my salvation. Not only does He *give* me strength to move forward... He *is* my strength. He makes me leap – like a deer – for joy!

In the book of Philippians, the apostle Paul adds to this insight.

"Rejoice in the Lord always; again I will say, rejoice" (Philippians 4:4 ESV).

In the light of Philippians, the quotation I used in opening this section makes perfect sense. Joy does not depend on my suffering – or the absence thereof. Joy depends on the fact that I know the Lord God saves me, remains present with me, and carries me through every event in life – no matter how difficult life may be.

Yet another absolutely incredible fact about joy comes from knowing the presence of God. In *Merriam-Webster's Collegiate Dictionary* definition, joy depends on earthly success, accomplishment, and circumstance. This world holds so many uncertain variables. Caleb's injury conveys an example of uncertain variables. If my joy rests on everything in my life being positive, that is a recipe for disaster in this world. Every human being experiences loss, pain, and failure. We might as well remove *joy* from the dictionary all together because *no one* would be able to grasp it. But if my joy rests in an unmovable, loving, powerful God, then nothing in this unstable world can steal that joy.

I will confess. The confident joy I write of does *not* come easily to me. My default mode for joy focuses on my circumstance and assigns my joy accordingly. But in my heart of hearts, I gratefully rejoice in the fact that joy can be mine simply by recognizing that God's presence in my life far outweighs any trial, failure, pain, or loss that I face. Joy is a matter of choice. By choosing to look toward the One who *is* joy, I receive the ability to live in joy, regardless of what my circumstance may be.

Chapter 8

Long Road to Recovery

CR

Sunday, September 4, was a *huge* day. My Sunday morning routine included getting up early to bed-bathe Caleb and change his bedding. I sat Caleb on the couch while I changed his bedding. About 9:00 a.m., my Sunday morning helper arrived to help me finish up my morning routine and to allow me to take a shower before church. That morning, Caleb became *very* agitated. When my morning helper and I tried to move him back to the bed, he became angry and took a slow swing at the helper. Then he spoke! Although the slurred mumble was hard to interpret, I thought he said, "Don't help me!" For some reason, he only wanted me to help him, but that frustration had been the key to initiate a vocalizing of words!

I felt sad for our helper because I sensed she felt a bit surprised, and I knew of no rational reason Caleb should have this response. However, at this point in time, he was not always rational. I believe he still saw most experiences through a fog, similar to coming out of a bad dream. He said, "Mom" and tried to speak more, but his words were jumbled. With this new development, Andy and I decided that he would stay with Caleb that morning while I went to church with Josh and Sarah. Although these first vocalizations seemed to sprout out of fear and frustration, the first attempts at verbalizing sparked new hope and opened another door toward clear communication.

We faced another slow process of relearning. Most of the time Caleb's words were so garbled that I could not understand. I often had to ask him to repeat, and those requests seriously frustrated him. To relieve some frustration and turn the focus off his inability and on to mine, I calmly explained that I was trying very hard to understand but needed him to be patient and help me. I found it remarkable that he could become irritated with situations and other people who were unfamiliar to him, but normally, he responded well to me and worked patiently to help me understand. Within a few days of the initial mumbles, he started uttering actual words to communicate.

Wonderful as it was to hear Caleb articulate words to communicate, most his efforts grew out of response to frustration and were only partially expressed through actual words. When he didn't like a therapist physically manipulating his body or pushing him to work harder, he told me to, "Make her leave!" Much of his therapy was difficult and even painful at times, but we had to interpret his feelings from "coded" reactions.

One example of my learning curve happened on a day he seemed resistant during a therapy session. Even though he asked me to "make her leave", he compliantly continued to work as I coaxed him. After a few more exercises, I asked what he wanted to do next. Using only hand motions, he pointed to his bed, but I failed to understand why he made that choice. Did he want to watch TV? Listen to music? Rest? He nodded 'yes' to rest; he was not giving up, he just needed a break. Suddenly, I realized uncovering his needs required keen observation of his body language paired with simple clarification questions in order to grasp his non-verbal cues. This early communication stage was a difficult and often frustrating process of trial and error... for Caleb and for me.

It is tough to explain the physical toil required in these early rehab sessions. Caleb worked about thirty minutes on standing, stepping, throwing a small ball, stretching... and then he would be completely wrung out. He often slept after only a half hour session because it took great physical effort for him to form words or to perform simple fine-motor skills. The therapy time for each day really only totaled about two to three hours of activity, but this effort drained all his energy. Here was a young man who used to thrive on daily weight training, individual skills training, and two hour evening basketball practice after a day of school and chores. Now, simple tasks of speaking, standing, and drawing taxed him to exhaustion.

Speech therapy took on a more intense purpose. Caleb showed strong retention of math skills. He began to use complete sentences, "More green Popsicle, please," as he was prompted. He did not like doing mental challenges but did show progress. One morning as Caleb sat in his wheelchair working on some mental games with the speech therapist, he became quite frustrated. He began to cry and pleaded with me to get her to leave. I had to leave the room so the therapist could get his attention.

It became more and more the case that I had to leave during some therapy sessions. When Caleb faced adversity or pain, he asked me to intervene and get rid of the therapist. I did not want him to feel I had deserted him, but he had to do the work, and it was, of course, natural for him to look to me to "save" him from the trial. Thankfully, as time went on, he became more willing to work. This rough phase lasted only a few weeks, and after that time, he worked very hard to recover. In fact, he often worked harder than asked in order to improve. He displayed a driven purpose to push himself as far as possible.

Caleb's ability to eat real food steadily improved. He could manage drinks and many soft foods... mashed potatoes, bananas, soft noodles. I felt grateful that he handled so much food because he quickly became intolerant of the formula fed through his G-tube. On September 14, he vomited his 6:00 p.m. feeding even though he showed no symptoms of illness; he just could not tolerate the formula. This intolerance to formula is common for many patients, and his vomiting increased over the next few days. Since his ability to manage foods continued to improve, I drastically decreased his formula quantity and filled his calorie count with regular food.

September revealed recovery progress on a daily basis; I acknowledged great victory in small events which would have gone unnoticed in my previously "normal" life. One mid-September evening, Caleb wanted to sit at the dinner table with us, so we helped him into his wheelchair and wheeled him up to the dinner table. Our menu that evening consisted of bread sticks and pizza. While Caleb could not eat pizza, he was able to feed himself bread sticks and hold his own cup as he drank some Coke. At this point, Caleb's senses were in "overdrive". Consequently, he loved the taste of food. He repeated over and over again, "This is *so* good!" As we all smiled, I realized how significant it was to have our family back at the table together for a meal. We still faced many trials and struggles on the road to recovery, but we recognized the significance of having our family united again and being on a path of restoration.

Prepared by God

"...And who knows whether you have not come to the kingdom for such a time as this?" Esther 4:14b (ESV).

As a Biblical narrative, the book of Esther holds a distinctive attribute in that the name of God is not mentioned even once in the book. Yet, as the story unfolds, God's orchestration of the events of the story becomes obvious. Let me briefly summarize the events of this narrative.

Esther, a Jew, lives in Susa, the capital city of ancient Persia. Because of an act of rebellion, the queen, Vashti, faces exile and loses her position as queen. Consequently, the king gathers many beautiful women into his harem with the intent of finding a new queen. Now, Esther is stunning... not only in physical beauty, but in beauty of spirit. She wins favor with many residents of the court... and she wins the favor of the king. Eventually, the king crowns her as his queen.

All this time, Esther keeps her nationality hidden. But after her coronation, the evil Haman manipulates the king into signing an order to exterminate the Jews. Prompted by her relative, Mordecai, Esther prepares to go to the king to beg for mercy. In Persia, an act of going unsummoned to the king held a penalty of death, even for the queen. Either way, she is dead. If she goes without being summoned, she could be executed; if she does not plead for mercy, she will suffer the same fate as all the Jews – death. At this point, Mordecai speaks a profound word that implies God has chosen Esther for this exact moment in time, "...who knows whether you have not come to the kingdom for such a time as this?"

Of course, Esther goes to the king. Haman's evil plot is revealed, and Haman is hung on the very gallows he built for the Jews.

Why have I included this account? Esther, although a stunning woman, was nothing more than a political captive from a conquered country. And yet, even from the moment of her capture and relocation, God was preparing her to save her people.

Sometimes when we face overwhelming circumstances, we easily go down the path of believing our circumstances are "unexpected". But nothing is unexpected for God. From His vantage point – timelessness – He sees everything that has come, is come, and will come. He may not stop an occasion from coming, but He is not surprised by it. How is this comforting to me? This knowledge comforts me because I can bank on the fact that He is preparing me today for what I will face tomorrow.

Looking back now, I see how God, the Master Conductor, prepared me for "such a time as this." As a child, I considered becoming a teacher. After graduating from high school, I felt uncertain about that career path. But after a year away from school, I felt renewed passion to pursue a degree in education. I worked hard, and after graduation I applied for and received my teaching certificate. Before we married, Andy and I agreed that I would stay home with children if the Lord blessed us with little ones. Well, He blessed us sooner than we expected, and Joshua was born ten months after our wedding. As a result, I did not pursue a teaching position. Two years later, Caleb arrived on the scene, and Sarah followed two years after Caleb. As Josh approached school age, we met another family who homeschooled their children. Despite the fact homeschooling was a completely new concept to me, I decided to explore the option. Surprisingly, even with holding a teaching certificate, I felt little confidence to homeschool our children. How could I care for two pre-school children, keep the house clean, prepare meals, *and* homeschool? But Andy supported me, and we decided to try it for one year.

Eventually, we homeschooled all three children. That preparation impacted my ability to handle Caleb's injuries in ways I could not imagine. When we began homeschooling, it was still a pretty novel idea. Homeschool laws in Washington gave parents a strong autonomy, but we were still thought to be a little peculiar. And perhaps we are... but... one thing I will say for homeschoolers... we learn to think outside the box and challenge the "norm". When Andy and I married, I would not have called myself a confident person... I'm not sure I would call myself confident today. But as a homeschool mom, I learned well the lesson to think outside the box. I also learned well not to cave in when pressured to conform.

When we began looking into options to take Caleb home while still in a coma, we faced resistance from the medical community. I am sure they feared we would hold them responsible if anything worse happened to Caleb. They really pressed us to move him to a long-term care nursing facility. Very few nursing facilities will take adolescents with Traumatic Brain Injury, but I managed to locate and visit two locations in our area. I complied with the suggestion to explore the long-term care services, but it only took a few moments of touring each facility to discourage me from choosing one of these two options. While most of the professional staff involved with our case continued to advise me toward the standard step of long-term residences, I drew on two skills learned through homeschooling: consider unconventional solutions and advocate for my own children. I needed both tools to fight for the goal we hoped to accomplish. God used homeschooling to prepare me to challenge the system and get Caleb home. That decision was a turning point in his recovery. Having constant contact with familiar people is believed to be a powerful stimulus in breaking through to patients in coma. Though I will never know for sure the differing impact between bringing Caleb home and taking him to a nursing facility, we believe that having Caleb home played a vital role in his eventual "waking".

Whether through my training as an educator, my years as a homeschool mom, or my God-given personality, I am a keen observer. Bringing Caleb home required me to quickly learn how to care for him. I learned to take and record vital signs, administer nutrition and water through a gastrointestinal tube, and regulate and administer a variety of medications. To be honest, before I took the plunge to go against the norm and homeschool, I doubt I would have possessed the courage to take on the primary care needs of a teenager in a coma. By the time we faced Caleb's injury, I was not fazed by marching to the beat of a different drummer. Sure, I needed and appreciated people who told me "you can do it", but the courage to take that step had been planted, nurtured, and grown by the experiences God led me through.

When Caleb finally headed back to school, he entered the classroom far below grade level. Again, homeschooling gave us an advantage. Dropping back into a role of teacher with him presented no problem at all. I felt confident to guide his path back to grade level, *and* the fact that he could draw on experience with me as his teacher for so many years gave us an instant rapport as teacher-student.

Homeschooling was a positive experience God used to shape me. But He also used a difficult negative experience to shape me. My family of origin was and is very close, but I had a brother who was less than ideal. He held serious anger issues, and those expressions of anger could be threatening. In my teen years, I attended counseling to deal with fear issues. The counseling I received paired with the experience of living with a manipulative, dishonest person gave me real life training in psychology. While Caleb and I worked through his rehab, some of the counseling staff told me that I was a "natural counselor" and had good intuition on how to work with him from an interpersonal perspective. Though some aspects of my childhood produced profoundly negative conditions, God redeemed those trials by molding me into the mother I needed to be when I took on the varied tasks of helping Caleb recover.

Now as I look back, it is crystal clear to me. From the time I was about seven years old, God began preparing me for the day when I would take a leap of faith and bring home a fifteen year old boy in a coma. God prepared me to counsel, coach, and teach that boy in order to assist him in his recovery. I may not have seen the storm coming, but God did. And He had in place every skill I would need when the time came that I needed to use them.

Chapter 9

September: A Month of Mental, Social, Physical, and Emotional Healing

CR

Brain injuries often result in significant damage to memory centers. Short term memory issues are pretty standard, but long term memories are usually preserved since these centers are more deeply situated in the brain. While Caleb suffered (and still does) from some short term memory issues, I routinely felt surprise at his long term memory. A prime example happened one day when I asked Caleb if he wanted to watch TV. He nodded 'yes', but since his speech was still quite difficult to understand, he repeated his request several times before I knew he wanted to watch a Chicago Bulls vs. Utah Jazz basketball playoff game. When Caleb was younger, he loved the Chicago Bulls of the 1990s, so he had recorded and saved many of their games. I left the room to find the VCR tape, but the Bulls had played in so many championship seasons that I could not remember which year they had played the Jazz. Holding a handful of video tapes, I yelled to Josh, "Which year did the Bulls play the Jazz?" The response I heard was not what I expected. Before Josh could answer Caleb started yelling, "'98,'98,'98". I began to smile. Caleb was unable to walk, talk clearly, remember the past year... but he knew *exactly* which year the Bulls played the Jazz, and he made sure I selected the specific game of the series he wanted to watch!

Caleb still had no memory of the whole year prior to the accident. He remembered his 8th grade year in middle school, but his first year at high school was gone. However, the really remarkable thing was that he remembered all the people he had ever met... no matter when he had met them. Even as the fall term started and most of Caleb's friends were back in school, many visitors came each day. Caleb's speech continued to improve and as he became more vocal, he verbally interacted with his visitors. As various friends stopped by, Caleb acknowledged each person by name. At first, I thought he remembered all these people from middle school, but then I learned he met several of these friends in high school. As the students shared daily high school events, Caleb easily recalled the names of all the high school teachers they mentioned. He thought the teachers were from middle school since he did not remember attending high school, but he absolutely identified each teacher. With all the memory issues we battled, I was astonished to realize his memory remained intact for *every* person in his life. I believe this specific set of memories shows how important people are to Caleb. In spite of the fact basketball had been his life focus for several years, he did not remember any basketball events or tournaments from his 9th grade year... but *all* the people he met at school or through basketball were still in his memory.

We also experienced some unique healing in social interaction. Most brain injury survivors suffer "egocentric" behavior. This happens because the injured brain may trend toward "tunnel vision". A brain injury may block the ability to read emotions, reactions, and needs of others. It is not due to a lack of caring, but rather to a lack of ability to see needs others have. In contrast, Caleb exhibited far less egocentric behavior than was expected. In addition to remembering names, Caleb often asked visitors, "How are you?" or "Would you like something to drink?" Since his speech was so difficult to understand, many friends did not catch what he was asking, but he graciously played the host! Even in these early stages of awareness, he was thinking outside of himself. Several therapists reminded me that sensitivity to others is quite atypical for his type of injury. Again, God preserved a unique, special part of his brain that made Caleb who he is.

Physically, therapy became more difficult. Now that Caleb could take labored steps, it was time to push toward really walking. The room he stayed in had two arched entryways, providing a one way "track" around the lower portion of the house. Our physical therapist coaxed Caleb to walk "laps" from his bed, through the entryway and kitchen, and back to his bed. Caleb often resisted. It was exhausting work for him, but we pushed him to build muscle strength. The physical therapist also walked Caleb up and down the stairs to the second floor which was nerve wracking for me because Caleb's sketchy balance caused him to totter and wobble. When the physical therapist trained me to repeat the stair climbing exercise, I hesitated at first due to fear of falling with Caleb. However, with help from Andy or Josh, Caleb improved as he continued ascending and descending stairs.

Early walking steps also provided the opportunity for Caleb to work on the ability to use the bathroom again. At first, the process was reminiscent of training a small child as I routinely took Caleb to the bathroom to retrain his body to use the toilet. Not only did he have to gain control of bladder and bowels, he had to gain the strength to sit up alone. Many days, success meant nothing more than completing an exercise and task without falling. However, all those exercises slowly retrained his muscles, and we crossed new milestones in clusters.

September 19 marked a "red-letter-day" of significant improvement. First, Caleb accomplished not only control over bladder and bowels but also strength to sit upright without assistance: a new freedom for him and me! I still walked him to the bathroom, assisted him to sit, and steadied him to stand again, but he was able to sit alone and use the toilet. Second, fine motor skills suddenly came around, and he managed to use a fork.

Although holding and manipulating the small tool still presented a challenge, we considered this improvement a spring-board step. Third, bringing new healing to my heart, this day shone with his first smile and small laugh!

The smile and laugh represented personality restoration, and those events cannot be overstated. The previous day, a girl had followed several friends around school and filmed a DVD for Caleb. Of course, some of the kids were goofing around and acting silly in front of the camera. As Caleb watched the clips on September 19, a funny scene happened and he actually smiled. Later that afternoon, we worked on one of our more challenging leg strengthening exercises. First, I sat Caleb on the edge of the couch. Next, I assisted him up and down as he performed basic squats next to the couch. Now, I agree, this must have looked ridiculous! I struggled to hold his weight as he did the squat. I did this next to the couch for good reason. As I faced Caleb, trying to hold him steady, I lost my balance, fell forward, and practically pushed him onto the couch. Caleb's reaction was a small, quiet, under-his-breath chuckle. "You think that is funny?" I asked. He chuckled and nodded, acknowledging his humor over my awkward fall. What a joy that brought to my heart! This laugh was so small it could have been easily missed, but considering this was Caleb's first laugh in three months, words seem shallow in expressing how moving it was to hear that small chuckle. Prior to this one significant day of progress, the in-home therapists had voiced doubt that Caleb would exhibit enough improvement to transition into the intense rehab slated for September 26. All skepticism fell away as the events of that one critical day launched us toward our next goal of in-patient rehab at Children's Hospital in Seattle.

This last week before intense rehab signified remarkable improvement in three crucial areas. As we hit each of these landmarks, Caleb continued to move forward with progress. First, after this initial day using the bathroom, he was consistent with the ability to let me know when he needed the bathroom. Second, his walking greatly improved, and although he was "herky-jerky", he could walk on his own. We always stayed close to him in case he fell, but we began walking all over the house and outside around the yard. The yard led to additional skills to master as he walked on the uneven grass surface, and every time we pushed further, he did remarkably well. Third, this was the week Caleb became completely intolerant of the formula fed through his G-tube, and he vomited within a matter of minutes after each feeding. I tracked and increased his calorie intake using regular foods. By the end of the week, he was able to eat many foods: mashed potatoes, chicken, and pasta. Renewed muscle strength even allowed him to sit on the couch and eat at a folding table rather than from his bed. By the time we headed to Children's, Caleb had completed a full week of meeting caloric needs through only oral consumption without formula supplement. Soaring upward with physical improvement, Caleb was ready for the intense therapy waiting at Children's Hospital.

However, we still faced emotional obstacles during this final week. His anxiety level intensified as the comfort and familiarity of home would soon be replaced by the unknown of living at the hospital. He begged to go just for day trips to the hospital and to come home at night, but we knew he would improve more quickly with intense resident therapy. Caleb showed some relief when he learned I planned to spend the entire first week with him and stay each night. Although he seemed more accepting of the transition, he told us he would only stay for one week. We knew the expectation was four to six weeks of therapy, but we gave him a small goal to focus on just one week... or even one day... at a time. "Let's just get through the first week, and then we'll see how it is going."

One morning during that last week at home, Caleb started asking me questions about North Bend, the high school, and places he was having trouble remembering. He had not left our house in two months, and that coupled with the loss of memory of the previous year left him with the need to put some of the scrambled pieces together. I suggested we take a "drive down memory lane". Josh and Sarah were at school, so I helped Caleb get into the front seat of the van. We drove all over North Bend... past familiar places. He saw the middle school and the high school. Seeing familiar sites helped him remember little events of times with friends at the local movie theater or restaurants. The little excursion lasted only about one hour, but we both enjoyed helping him uncover memories of the past.

A severe brain injury can leave a victim with difficulty processing large amounts of sensory input at any one time. Large crowds present especially overwhelming and disturbing sensory overload with a bombardment of sights, sounds, and smells. Again, Caleb's reaction did not follow the norm for a brain injury. On Friday, September 23, we witnessed Caleb thrive in a large group of people.

During the summer, our high school underwent a huge upgrade and remodel to the entire sports complex. The gymnasium was improved and expanded, and beautiful new football/soccer stadium, softball/baseball fields, and track facilities opened the fall of 2005. On September 23, the first home football game of the year included a stadium dedication event. A friend had contacted the high school athletic director, and they discussed having Caleb attend and participate in the celebration events. Our rehab team warned us that large crowds and noise can severely disturb an individual with a serious brain injury since the patient cannot adequately filter the bombardment of sensory input that most of us handle every day. Our local high school and small town community had tremendously supported Caleb over the past months, and we wanted to give them a chance to share in Caleb's remarkable progress. After consideration, we agreed to give it a try and take Caleb to the game.

On Friday night, we loaded up the wheelchair and drove to the stadium. We live in a one high school community, and the school grounds were packed. We found it difficult to find parking near the stadium, and by the time we finally got Caleb wheeled onto the football field, the dedication activities were already beginning.

The editor of the local newspaper was the Master of Ceremonies for the event, and as we rolled in, he introduced Caleb and mentioned his remarkable recovery. Caleb sat in the wheelchair as the people in the stands cheered and rose to their feet to recognize Caleb. He waved to them as Andy and I stood in the background and again marveled at the support Caleb received from our community. Caleb's reaction was far from unsettled. He waved to the stands and seemed completely at ease with the loud applause from the standing-room-only crowd. After the opening ceremonies, I thought it might be best to keep Caleb away from so much commotion, so I took him to the far end of the stadium where the crowd was small. Shortly after we settled far from the hubbub, Caleb became restless being so far from the people... he asked to be in the middle of all the activity. As I wheeled him around the grounds, many people came to wish him well. I didn't even know all the people who stopped us. Caleb *loved* every moment, and we stayed for the entire football game. Caleb hardly saw a play, but he flourished in all the activity and contact with people.

After the good reaction to the football crowd, we felt comfortable to take Caleb to church for the first time since the accident. People at our church knew of the plan to transition to Children's the next day and of Caleb's anxiety over the relocation. Still cautious of Caleb becoming overwhelmed around people and noise, we wheeled him in and sat in the very back of the church. Just a few minutes into the service, our pastor asked Caleb to come forward. Caleb wanted to walk up on his own, so Andy and I followed him as he slowly and laboriously walked to the front.

Astounding everyone, Caleb walked all the way to the front on his own power. He did still lack endurance, and he asked to sit in his wheelchair once he made it to the front of the church. Our pastor reminded everyone that Caleb was scheduled to begin intense rehab the next day, and pastor suggested that the body gather around Caleb to pray. We wheeled Caleb into the center aisle as people circled around him. Several people began to pray, and Caleb heard prayers for his strength, peace, growth, improvement, and release from concern and fear. After the prayer time closed, Caleb looked up, saw everyone standing around him, and simply said, "Thanks guys." Those two words stuck in my mind because he was thinking past himself and showing gratefulness to others for their support... again very much unlike most brain-injured patients.

After church that day, we hosted a big farewell barbeque at our home as several of the moms of friends had arranged a send-off. They contacted Caleb's high school friends and prepared all the food, and God blessed us with a beautiful, sunny day. On the deck in his wheelchair, Caleb chatted with many friends gathered around as over forty people came throughout the day. Caleb ate hot dogs, visited with friends, and thoroughly enjoyed interacting with everyone.

It was a fantastic weekend. We had enjoyed the Friday night game and the honor of participating in the dedication. The Sunday morning gathering with our church family and the afternoon barbeque with many well-wishers were both wonderful events to send us on our way in the next phase of the journey.

Miracles

"And He answered and said to them, 'Go and report to John what you have seen and heard: the blind receive sight, the lame walk, the lepers are cleansed, and the deaf hear, the dead are raised up, and the poor have the gospel preached to them'" Luke 7:22 (NASB).

Do miracles happen today? *Merriam-Webster's Collegiate Dictionary* defines miracle as, "an extraordinary event manifesting divine intervention in human affairs."[1] To this day, we find it difficult to explain Caleb's healing without looking to some kind of divine hand in the process. At the very least, Caleb's recovery is consistent with a more modern definition of *miracle* found on dictionary.com: "An effect or extraordinary event in the physical world that surpasses all known human or natural powers and is ascribed to a supernatural cause."[2] For people who did not experience the injury and recovery phases first hand, it may be difficult to fully understand the depth of the injury in relation to the extent of his recovery. I will try to give a glimpse of what we faced and what *should* have been the outcome for Caleb.

Traumatic brain injuries and comas are assessed by a standard called the Glasgow Coma Scale. This scale evaluates visual, motor, and verbal responses to stimuli, and each response, or lack of response, is scored. When the scores from each category are added, the total Glasgow Coma Scale score helps doctors identify a person's consciousness and extent of brain injury. This scale shows remarkable consistency even when various

1. By permission. From *Merriam-Webster's Collegiate® Dictionary, 11th Edition* ©2014 by Merriam-Webster, Inc. (www.Merriam-Webster.com)
2. "miracle." *Dictionary.com Unabridged.* Random House, Inc. Web. 20 Oct. 2014. <Dictionary.com http://dictionary.reference.com/browse/miracle>.

healthcare professionals perform the evaluation and assign the scoring. The scale runs from 3-15, and a lower score indicates more severe brain injury and poorer prognosis.

To give some perspective, here are a few facts on the scoring. Patients with a score equal to or greater than 9 are not in a coma. A score of 13-15 normally indicates minor injury, and a score of 9-12 usually indicates moderate severity. Patients with a score equal to or less than 8 are in a coma. A score below 3 indicates a vegetative state and is compatible with brain death. Therefore, 8 is the critical scoring point. Scores from 3-8 normally result in severe disability. With a score below 8 at six hours after injury, only 50% of patients survive.

Caleb's score was a 6. Not only was Caleb at a 6 just hours after the injury, he was at a 6 for *weeks* after the injury. A score of 6 implies a wide range of long-term consequences and disabilities. First of all, Caleb had only a 50% chance of surviving and living past the injury. But even with surviving the injury, there is a long list of "should haves". Caleb should:

- need a wheelchair;

- struggle with severe speech impediments;

- face mental disability;

- battle emotionally immaturity;

- require maintenance medication to balance neurological activity, emotional stability, or even seizures.

For each of these "should haves", the opposite is true:

- Caleb is alive!

- Caleb can walk, run, and ride a bike.

- Although he battles some minor speech and language concerns, most people do not notice speech issues unless they are made aware of the injury.

- Caleb graduated from high school with honors *and* from college with a bachelor's degree.

- Everyone has emotional challenges, and Caleb is no different, but he is remarkably balanced in spite of the injury. He does not suffer from volatile anger, isolation, or depression.

- Once we weaned Caleb off the "cocktail" of drugs he came home with, he has needed *no* maintenance medication whatsoever.

Caleb is an anomaly!

Recently, a friend asked me if Caleb has been evaluated for disability. He did undergo two sets of evaluations. One took place after four weeks of intense rehab at Children's, and a second set of evaluations was performed about four months after discharge from rehab. Caleb's evaluation scores did improve over time, but the scores still showed significant deficits. However, the evaluators did notice that Caleb's functionality went beyond what the test scores indicated. I was told that functionality is the *true* evaluation tool. If Caleb functions beyond the score indicators, then we are in uncharted territory.

Another barrier to brain injury recovery is that brain and neurological tissue does not fully heal after being damaged. When a person breaks a bone, the bone tissue can rebuild itself, often becoming even sturdier than before the break. When a sharp object cuts into a person's skin, the body regenerates and heals the damaged skin and underlying blood vessels. However, neurological tissue does not fully regenerate, and once brain tissue is damaged or injured, it loses the full extent of its previous functionality. Nevertheless, some research shows that adjacent brain tissue will take over the function of damaged tissue. Of course, this can only happen to a limited extent since neurological tissue and brain regions possess specific purposes. But in the end, healing primarily happens as undamaged tissue takes on the duty of the damaged tissue.

So how can I explain the anomaly of Caleb's functionality? Even the medical community struggles to adequately explain the outcome. Is his recovery a miracle? Some people may say it is not a miracle in the Biblical sense of the word. However, for me to explain how Caleb moved from a Glasgow score of 6 to graduating from college and living on his own, I can only say that God chose to heal Caleb beyond what was reasonably expected. Merriam-Webster's definition as "an extraordinary event manifesting divine intervention in human affairs" does seem to describe Caleb's healing.

We live in such a technologically advanced society that it is easy to miss or belittle the every-day wonders around us. Don't we all experience aspects of life around us which seem impossible to explain from a human perspective? The birth of a baby, the metamorphosis of a butterfly, the starlit sky on a clear night, the perfect cycle of the ocean tides, the interconnectedness of plant and animal life... the very existence, protection, and maintenance of each "simple" example screams of the intervention of a supernatural power.

Beyond those wonders is another more surprising wonder. Divine intervention implies intimate personal interaction originating *from* the Divine. It is so simple for me to feel like an insignificant speck in the scope of history, time, and space, and yet Divine intervention bestows significance on me. Divine intervention is God's continuous, intimate connection to my life. Now, that is a miracle which surpasses my limited human understanding! God, who is vast enough to hold and direct the universe in His hand, extends immeasurable love to me and personally directs every aspect of my life.

I think that qualifies as "extraordinary... divine intervention in human affairs."

I believe Caleb's healing *is* a physical miracle. It qualifies as an unexpected occurrence in the physical world that goes beyond human understanding and must be ascribed to a supernatural power... God. But beyond that physical miracle is a miracle of God-instigated, ongoing, intimate relationship between Jesus and Caleb... between Jesus and me... between Jesus and you, if you accept it.

Chapter 10

Rehab

CR

On Monday, September 26, 2005, Caleb and I headed to Seattle Children's Hospital for rehab. Although we had been talking about this trip and preparing him for the transition, he still felt less than positive about this venture. Unfortunately, even with the therapists' efforts to persuade Caleb that this rehab was a great opportunity for him to improve, he was not convinced. He kept telling me he would only stay one week. I knew the rehab team expected a four to six week plan, but Caleb could only handle small goals. So I told him just to get through the first week and then we could decide from there. Although he still disliked the idea, Caleb gave me no trouble as I loaded him, his wheelchair, and our bags into the van.

Because of Caleb's uncertainty and fear, I hoped Children's would place us in a private room rather than a double occupancy room. There were no private rooms available on the day we arrived; however, our assigned double room had no other patient. So we were able to have the whole large room to ourselves. This was a welcomed relief for me, and the opportunity for us to enjoy more relaxed private time helped both of us adjust to the rehab situation.

From the first week at Harborview, I looked forward to the day we could transfer to Children's for intense therapy. It represented a profound step back toward recovery for Caleb. Now that we had arrived, I was ready for Caleb to jump right in with the therapy, and I expected to begin the first day with several hours of work. However, the first day revolved around evaluations with several therapists. Although Caleb had completely converted to a solid food diet, the Children's speech therapist was required to evaluate Caleb before he could eat regular food at the hospital. During the evaluation, she tested Caleb's ability to handle several food consistencies, including the final test of Doritos. If he could handle the sharp, crunchy corn chips, he could eat anything he wanted. He did well, and he was cleared to eat all foods. This was wonderful! For several weeks now, he anticipated eating popcorn, and on this first night at Children's, we had popcorn! This therapist also completed an evaluation on Caleb's speech abilities. Although I could understand most of his communication by now, significant impediment still impacted his speech. After further evaluations with the occupational therapist and physical therapist, we had short, thirty minute rehab sessions with each of the three therapists in the afternoon.

One real highlight of the first day at Children's was a shower. Since I had no way of safely bathing him at home even after he began to regain mobility, I had continued daily bed baths in Caleb's personal hygiene routine. At Children's, Caleb's private bath included a shower area large enough to accommodate a wheelchair, and the shower floor was simply an extension of the main tile floor. We requested a regular plastic chair, and Caleb sat in the spray of warm water while I helped him take his first shower in over three months. A shower may seem like an odd thing to be excited about, but bed bathing a teen-age boy is difficult and not very private. The independence to take a real shower removed one more shackle restricting us from normal life, and we gratefully enjoyed each regained freedom, no matter how small.

On Tuesday, the therapy plan began to reflect our schedule for the next few weeks. Caleb and I had approval to independently take on his personal morning routine of shower and breakfast. A large whiteboard near the nurse's station displayed the daily rehab schedule for every patient in the ward. One of Caleb's tasks each morning was to write his schedule in a journal. During the day, we attended seven thirty-minute sessions. Two sessions were scheduled for each area of speech therapy, occupational therapy, and physical therapy, and one session was spent with a school teacher. When we had free time, we worked together on any assignments Caleb received from the school teacher. I appreciated the opportunity to become an active part of the rehab process. Each therapist welcomed me to sit in on sessions, to take notes, and to learn as much as I could in order to continue working with Caleb once he was discharged.

I knew Caleb was not thrilled to be at Children's. I did expect that once we got there, he would see his own improvement and be more amiable about staying until the completion of rehab. But even on the first day, Caleb asked if he could go home to see the high school football game on Friday. To my surprise, the doctors said it might be something we could do. I hoped they were not giving him false hope, but I learned their goals were to do everything possible to get him back into his teen life. The therapy schedule ran Monday through Saturday morning, but doctors suggested that we might be allowed to go home each Saturday afternoon and return each Sunday night. They were also willing to give him an evening pass to attend the Friday night football games *if* he worked hard. The hope of short reprieves from the hospital gave Caleb a goal and helped him push harder in his therapy. Caleb knew the doctors would be keeping an eye on his progress and that his hard work might offer him the opportunity to go to the game.

By the end of the first week, he showed marked improvement. The doctors agreed to give him an evening pass for Friday night, but they reminded Caleb that he could go only if he agreed to come back the same night without giving me a hard time. He agreed. After dinner, Caleb and I drove out to the football game at our high school. He loved being with his friends, and again, he did very well around all the activity.

Throughout the first week at Children's, I persistently asked the doctors to remove Caleb's G-tube. The short tube sticking out of his abdominal region just above the belly button really hindered some of his therapy because he could not lay on his stomach with this tube in the way. Our head doctor was working on the situation, but the doctors in charge of removing the tube said Caleb could not have it removed. When the tube was inserted at Harborview, I was told the tube must stay for six weeks to allow proper healing of the hole it made in his stomach. Now the gastroenterologists were saying it had to stay for a couple more months! This was so disappointing! The doctor leading our rehab team did not give up; he assertively asked the gastroenterology team to come evaluate Caleb. By Friday night, we were still waiting for an evaluation. After the football game, Caleb and I returned to his room about 10:30 p.m. As soon as we walked onto the rehab floor, the nurses sent us off to radiology. The radiology tech had stayed late so that she could perform a scan of Caleb's abdominal area to give the doctors a clear look at the tube insertion area. Caleb and I were scheduled to go home for the weekend after his Saturday morning therapy, and before we left for the weekend, the gastroenterologist came into Caleb's room and reported that the scan showed he could remove Caleb's tube. As he snipped the end of the tube, the air escaped from the tiny internal balloon which secured the tube. The doctor easily pulled out the tube and Caleb felt no pain. We were so excited to go home on that first Saturday with the tube gone! There was a slight hole in Caleb's skin, but by evening, it was already closing. He has a scar to this day, but it just looks like he has two belly buttons!

We both felt grateful to be home for the weekend. Attending church on Sunday provided a source of strengthening for us and a blessing to our church family. This was only the second time Caleb had been able to go to church since the accident in June. On Sunday night, the five of us went to dinner as a family and took Caleb back to Children's. The plan was to drop Caleb at the hospital on Sunday night, and then I would return on Monday morning. Caleb still felt quite fearful of being alone at the hospital; he pleaded with me to stay. The fear of being there alone was so intense that he started to sob. The sound of his very deep voice in so much turmoil was more than I could take. Sarah could not stand to see him this way; she left the room sobbing and joined Andy and Josh in the hallway. I went into the hall and saw Andy trying to comfort Sarah. It took only a few moments for us to see it would be best for me to stay. Because we had planned for me to go home, I did not have any clothes or overnight supplies. When Sarah got home that evening, she packed a bag for me, and friends brought my things the next day. From that point on, I stayed at Children's with Caleb, and the two of us went home together on the weekends.

I am a teacher by profession. At the time, I had a one-day-a-week teaching job at a homeschool cooperative. Two dear friends, Mary Kaye and Lisa, helped me keep my classes going while I was at Children's. On Wednesday evenings, one of them came to stay with Caleb so I could go home; finish preparing for classes; and see Andy, Josh, and Sarah. I taught my classes on Thursdays, and Mary Kaye or Lisa left the hospital after Caleb began his Thursday therapy sessions. By the time Caleb finished with all his sessions on Thursday afternoons, I had returned to the hospital. The precious time given by these two ladies allowed me to continue my part-time job and know that Caleb was not alone.

On the second Saturday that we were able to go home, Andy was coaching Sarah for a 1:00 p.m. soccer game in Snoqualmie. Since Caleb received an early therapy schedule, we planned to go to her game before we went home. We arrived at the fields but had to park a fair distance from the game. Although Caleb had become more mobile, we still used the wheelchair to cover long distances, so I unloaded the wheelchair. However, on this day, Caleb wanted to try walking on his own from the parking lot to the team bleachers. As we slowly walked along the path, I pushed the empty chair in case he tired before we made it across the park. Since walking was still *very* jerky and labored, he had to walk very slowly, and I wasn't sure if he could keep his balance over rough terrain. But our continued goal was to let him take on whatever challenge he felt ready to attempt. Slowly and deliberately, he walked the whole distance of roughly a quarter mile over to the field. Such a short distance, but for him at this stage, it was fantastic. He stood for part of the game and took short rests to sit a bit, but after the game, he walked all the way back to the car. With such significant accomplishment after only two weeks of in-patient therapy, we decided to return the wheelchair to the supply company. From then on, Caleb patiently continued to improve his walking skills and never used a wheelchair again.

By our third week at Children's, the therapy team increased the length of most of his sessions. Each day included one thirty and one forty-five minute session with each therapist, and the work intensified. Speech therapy included many mental games, memory techniques, word/vocabulary development, and actual speech improvement. Karen, the speech therapist, was a graduate of Washington State University and a Duke University fan. Caleb liked the University of Washington and North Carolina University – Michael Jordan's alma mater. He loved giving Karen a bad time, and she played along teasing him back. Occupational therapy exercises targeted fine motor skills to improve basic life skills and to reduce the tension and spasticity in the right arm. Some of the exercises were fun and included games which required hand-eye coordination, agility, and speed. Caleb also enjoyed the chance to bake cookies and relearn the skills of reading and following directions on his own. Little did he know this activity was also a test to see if he could safely use the oven and stove in a kitchen. Physical therapy trained large motor skills as therapist Kristi spent time recovering balance and fluidity of movement. Caleb could walk, but it was still very jerky and labored, and he struggled to get his arms to swing normally as he walked. Kristi used two large poles and had him hold one in each hand. Holding the other ends of the poles, she stood behind Caleb. As they walked, she moved her own arms so that the poles moved Caleb's arms in the correct rhythm with his walking. His brain relearned the rhythm quickly, and he began to look less awkward in his gait. Caleb progressed quickly under the intensive therapy sessions, and he pushed hard with little to no frustration level.

Even with notable improvement, forward progress could still provoke painful feelings for Andy and me. One day during our third week, Andy came to visit. Caleb couldn't wait to show Andy that he could run again. When we thought of Caleb running, we pictured the agile, smooth, graceful athlete he had been – one who had the ability to bounce a basketball into the air, meet it at a ten foot rim, and dunk it. As Caleb awkwardly ran down the hall, Andy's face showed a painful tension between feelings of happiness and sadness. Caleb looked like a large, teen-age boy imitating a two year old who is trying to run for the first time. Yet, we both realized these clumsy and uncoordinated first efforts of running indicated a huge accomplishment. I don't think Caleb realized how awkward he looked. It didn't look anything like the way he ran only four months prior to this, but that did not seem to faze him. Overall, with each skill reacquired, he rejoiced and showed very little discouragement over the bumps in the path. When he felt frustrated, he shared that hurt but quickly moved on. He was determined to "get better" and no matter what the therapists asked him to do, he worked hard to accomplish and go beyond their expected goals. His positive, never-quit attitude can *only* be explained as a gift from God!

Pain and Perseverance

"For I know the plans I have for you, declares the Lord, plans for welfare and not for evil, to give you a future and a hope" Jeremiah 29:11 (ESV).

Caleb attacked his rehab with determination to improve and recover as much as possible. He encountered moments when the therapy was physically very painful, but he pushed on anyway. In fact, sometimes, the pain motivated him to work all that much harder. As we explored ways to expand and enhance rehab services for Caleb, two wonderful men stepped forward and volunteered to work with Caleb. Ryan and Nate spent several hours every week working with Caleb at our local fitness club. Since both men came from intense sports backgrounds, they pushed Caleb hard, *very* hard. Caleb never complained. In fact, he once told Andy, "Ryan and Nate make me hurt, but I like it." How could he like the pain? He liked it because he knew that every painful step forward moved him closer to healing and retrieving his physical abilities. Even pain held no power to deter him from pushing himself to the limits of his abilities to recover and grow.

While I could chalk up this determination to his athletic training and skills, I believe Caleb's determination goes beyond a simple humanistic determination. Caleb holds to a secure belief that God has a purpose for his life. I see this play out in his life over and over again.

Life is just tough at times. Add a brain injury to the already difficult circumstances of life, and discouragement waits to bubble to the surface. I am continually amazed at how Caleb faces adversity. When he struggles with discouragement, it normally only lasts a few hours; then he just comes back with, "I'm not worried. God always provides a way."

I could learn from that attitude. I worry and fret. As if my worry and fret can rectify the situation, I mull over all the possible outcomes – even when the outcome is out of my control. Of course there are times we have to take action. Caleb did not lay in his bed waiting for God to magically restore his muscles, coordination, speech, mental processing, etc. He got up and pushed himself, and when he fell down, he got up again. He took direction from doctors and therapists who gave him a plan of attack. Not knowing whether his efforts would succeed or fail, he still aggressively worked to meet challenging goals. He took action. Pushing through the pain strengthened his physical muscles and pushing through adversity has strengthened his spiritual muscles. When life zings him with something outside his control, Caleb knows to trust God for the solution because he knows God is faithful and can be trusted to bring purpose into his life.

So how does that balance work? How can we be people who push to the limit of our abilities and still hold the outcome of the situation in an open hand? I'm not sure I have mastered this. On second thought, I am sure I have *not* mastered this! But I learn from observing this course with my son. I must take action. I consider various options and solutions to a problem. Then I set a plan of action and instigate that plan. But always underneath the plan must lay trust that God's purposes will be fulfilled, and those purposes do not rest on my perfect execution of my plan, on the seemingly insurmountable obstacles in the path, or on the pain along the way.

"Many are the plans in the mind of a man, but it is the purpose of the Lord that will stand" (Proverbs 19:21 ESV).

At first glance, this verse sounds like we make plans and God changes them. But actually, this is a comforting verse about His faithfulness. We make plans, put them in motion, and trust in the Lord. He will bring those plans to fruition, or not, but His purpose will always rise to the surface.

What is His purpose? Well, big picture... His purpose is that we have deep, intimate relationship with Him. His purpose is that we know He loves us beyond what we could possibly imagine. His purpose is that we trust Him to guide our lives and to provide all we need... need, not want. I must remember that my perspective of need may not be in line with His perspective of my need. My greatest need has been met because He has solved my greatest problem which was separation from Him. God will do whatever it takes to reach me with His unimaginable love and to restore my relationship with Him. And regardless of the curves life throws my way, since His purpose flows from His deep love for me, I too can say, "I'm not worried. God always provides."

God's initial intention is to restore His personal relationship with me, but once that bond is reinstated, He expands the purpose outward. He supplies a purpose for my life; a truly worthwhile purpose to touch the lives of other people. This thought boggles my mind... God does not need me to impact lives; He is certainly powerful enough to connect to every person on the planet without my help. But in order to bestow purpose into *my* existence, He entrusts me with a purpose to engage in meaningful experiences and relationships with people. Learning from my life experiences, I grow in order to minister to others and to impact the lives of people in need of support and compassion.

But don't forget, impact may mean a collision has occurred; impact can be painful! I may have to live through, or *in*, pain in order to accomplish long-term impact and change. People I love may have to live through or in pain as well. If I focus on the pain, I may give up or be crushed by its weight, but if I can focus on the beauty and strength that grows out of pain, I may be able to push forward and even embrace the pain. That does not mean the pain hurts less; there are times the pain is so excruciating that it flattens me. My "trainer", Jesus, often has to massage and stretch my emotional and spiritual muscles in order for me to get off the floor and back to the painful task. As I persevere and gain glimpses of the benefits of the pain, I gain a sense of hope for my future.

Chapter 11

Reintegrating into Life

ॐ

Throughout the initial months after the accident, both the Harborview staff and the home rehab team prepared us to accept possible loss of speech, motor skills, mental processes, and memory. However, the most disheartening possible consequence was that we may "lose" much of who Caleb was as a new personality emerged. Since Caleb suffered damage in the frontal lobe area of the brain, which is in part responsible for a person's decision making, planning, and problem solving, we were concerned his personality traits may change. Sadly, damage in the frontal lobe rarely produces more pleasant personalities but often causes people to react with more selfishness, discouragement, and negativity. This realization was painfully difficult for me to accept. Even from a young age, Caleb had been a person who enjoyed surrounding himself with others, shared an easy sense of humor, laughed often, and tuned in to the feelings of others. Few hardships discouraged him, and he frequently attacked struggles with confidence that he could overcome the issue. I found it hard to image him as a person void of these qualities.

But over time, we saw that while there were slight changes in his personality, new traits were not as negative as we had feared, and most of who he was before remained. Caleb's strong extrovert tendencies continued, and he still loved being around people. Age difference or lack of familiarity between Caleb and another person was no barrier for Caleb as he easily carried on conversations with anyone. His contagious laugh was triggered quickly, and he could even laugh at himself and the silly little things he did. Talking and losing his train of thought mid-sentence resulted in chuckles rather than anger. Sure, he faced moments of real grief and loss, but after the initial weeks of struggle, he approached his rehab and therapy with drive to improve. He was especially determined to get his physical strength and motor skills back. Therapists and trainers enjoyed Caleb's attitude and were quick to comment how wonderful it was to work with Caleb because he never complained about how hard the exercises were... he just pushed harder. Often sweating up a storm, he aggressively attacked each exercise in his goal to move onto tougher routines. Today, when people ask me if Caleb's personality is different compared to before the accident, I explain that although essentially the same, the traits from before – both good and bad – are now more intense and exaggerated. In spite of the heightened personality traits, the real essence of Caleb's fun-loving yet determined attitude still defines who he is, which is yet again another way that he is an anomaly and falls outside the normal expectations for recovery from a brain injury.

One of the many signs of this personality preservation happened one afternoon at Children's as Caleb lost his cool with me. For some reason, he seemed testy that afternoon. Snapping at me, he blurted out that I didn't want to help him and I didn't care. The tension of three weeks away from home was beginning to wear on me, and my composure failed under his sharp comment. As I started to tear up, all I could choke out was, "That is unfair. I care a great deal and have worked hard to help you recover." To my surprise, he immediately softened and apologized. Now, such a response would be atypical for even a normal fifteen year old boy. But add to the situation brain injury propensities toward great self-centeredness and very little intuitive awareness of emotional pain in someone else, and the softened response becomes even more unlikely. When I told the therapists about the incident, they expressed amazement. The fact that Caleb conveyed compassion for my feelings, recognized his part in hurting me, and apologized for his actions was really quite remarkable. Their encouraging words gave me hopeful expectations for recovery and preservation of his personality and interpersonal skills.

Part of his rehab included several sessions for recreational therapy such as off-site events. One day, we went out to pizza with the recreational therapist and Caleb's assigned intern. Caleb ordered and paid for the meal, making sure he paid accurately and received proper change. This outing provided a great time for him to converse and interact with the two ladies in our company – the therapist and our young intern. Another day, we went to a large Barnes and Nobel bookstore. Caleb was given $25 dollars (donated by a generous Children's supporter) with the assignment to look around the store, make his own selections, purchase the items, and check for proper payment and change. On that day, it just so happened that a group of five girls had come to visit. We were actually walking out to the van for our outing when we saw the girls in the lobby. The recreational therapist invited the girls to join us, and we all climbed into the van to make the Barnes and Nobel visit.

This unexpected visit presented a great opportunity for the therapist to see how Caleb interacted with others. He was very social and enjoyed the activity of strolling around the mall area. He chatted with the girls as they walked around looking in shop windows. As we walked, I discretely reminded him to watch for certain concerns – use the handrail on stairs, double-check change from the cashier, etc. He was quick to process and follow through with these simple reminders. The therapist was impressed with how well he handled the environment and interaction with his friends.

Such outings seem relatively simplistic and insignificant only because we tend to overlook the broad range of sensory and mental inputs people unconsciously assess at lightning speeds while interacting with places and individuals around us. It was truly remarkable that Caleb didn't really struggle to interact with people and places. He was completely relaxed and thoroughly enjoyed the experience. Caleb exhibited behaviors uncharacteristic of victims of a brain injury who are typically withdrawn and incapable of appropriately responding to the people around them. I did not overlook God's protection of Caleb's social personality.

Affliction and Suffering

"And not only this, but we also exult in our tribulations, knowing that tribulation brings about perseverance; and perseverance, proven character; and proven character, hope; and hope does not disappoint, because the love of God has been poured out within our hearts through the Holy Spirit who was given to us" Romans 5:3-5 (NASB).

I personally believe that every person goes through suffering – it is part of the human condition. While no one hopes for or enjoys suffering, there can be four positive results that grow out of suffering: Glory for God, good for others, growth for the sufferer, and credibility for the sufferer to share with others in similar situations. My suffering touches on all four of these realms.

Glory for God – Caleb manifests miraculous healing that can only be explained by the power of the divine. His type of brain injury nearly always results in some serious disability and need for monitoring. This short list explains consequences Caleb should face and the contrasting reality he lives in today:

- The need for medication to balance his brain activity – He is on *no* medication at all.

- Significant speech impediment – Although Caleb may slur slightly when he is tired, his overall speech is coherent and clear. Considering we were told he may not even understand verbal communication, let alone speak again, this is remarkable. He still possesses a functional vocabulary. The speech center of his brain suffered substantial damage, and yet, he not only speaks and understands speech... he majored in speech

111

communication in school. I think the irony of that fact must bring a smile to God's face!

- Physical disability – We expected him to be in a wheelchair. We were exploring treatment methods to relax the intense spasticity in his right arm – which eventually just released on its own. Fine motor skills showed noteworthy concern in the early stages of rehab and therapy, and though they still present the greatest physical challenge, they do not limit his activity. His balance is not what it was before the accident, but through hard work, his balance is better than some people who have never suffered a brain injury. An observant person will notice a bit of awkwardness in his gait, but this does not impact his mobility. He even runs on a treadmill without falling.

- Memory disability – He still deals with some short-term memory issues, but overall his memory functions above what is expected for those who suffer a brain injury.

So what does all this mean? The healing he experienced and still experiences goes beyond reasonable medical explanation. To me, the only answer I can come up with is to say that God healed Caleb. Why He chose to heal Caleb I cannot completely know. But the healing is for God's glory. He did it. He uses it. He deserves the praise.

Good for Others – I honestly cannot know how all of this has played out. But for years after the injury, others have been impacted by the events we lived through. While we were in the thick of the struggle, we saw high school students come together in a way rarely witnessed in that age group. Many students changed in ways that impacted their beliefs, attitudes, and behaviors. For some of the students, these changes shaped the way they grew into adulthood. Occasionally, I will run into one of these students in town when they are home to visit family. I still enjoy *big* hugs from many of those students, who are now adults. Even though I may only see these young people once every two or three years, there is a bond that goes beyond our proximity to each other. We share a life-changing, common experience that has defined our relationship in a way no other "lesser" experience could.

As people who live routine lives, we often forget how many other people we cross paths with. One example of this happened about a year after the injury. Andy began working for Costco soon after the injury happened. A few Costco employees we knew added Caleb to a prayer chain with some other employees. Months later, Andy learned of the fact that others at Costco had been following our story, so he sent an email update to those on the group list. He was overwhelmed with responses of people from all walks of life who shared the ways they had been impacted by the story. We did not know any of the people who responded to him, but many of them voiced significant personal impact from following the story. This is only one example. For years after the incident, we heard similar stories of people we had never known, from various parts of the country we have never visited.

"Is anyone among you suffering? Let him pray. Is anyone cheerful? Let him sing praise" (James 5:13 ESV).

Suffering is meant to be shared in order to bond people together and to offer support for those in need. The beautiful result is that when people have bonds in suffering, they also enjoy mutual celebration when it is time to rejoice.

There was one other remarkable and unexpected result of openly sharing our suffering with our local community. In any community, conflicts arise. People have contradictory opinions which can result in hard feelings and broken relationships. The reality is that competition can become a springboard for differences of opinion and conflict. Since we were heavily involved in the sports arena of our community, we had experienced some broken relationships over the years. However, I marveled to see how quickly hard feelings softened as we openly shared our tragedy with the community. People who had not spoken to us in years suddenly made a purposeful effort to speak to us. Many offered time and resources to help us in any way needed – installing handicap equipment in our home, working on yard maintenance for us, attending fundraisers to help with our medical costs. Other people actually came to us to intentionally heal relationships, as apologies and forgiveness were exchanged from both sides. The suffering we were living through tore down walls and defused long-time grudges. I personally have never experienced such relationship turnaround at any other point in my life.

Growth for the Sufferer – I would not wish my experience on any person. The uncertainty and fear was debilitating at times. However, I would not trade the growth I have seen in myself, Andy, Caleb, Josh, and Sarah. We are the people we are now not *in spite of* the suffering but *because of* the suffering. Andy and I both have a much deeper empathy and appreciation for any person who is suffering. We are both less judgmental of people as we realize we may have *no* idea what pain a person may be privately coping with. I think those traits are true for our children as well. In addition to that, all three of our children have been drawn to careers or volunteer work that serves people; all three highly value people and relationships. They all possess deeply rooted faith and beliefs that carry them through trials. I have been amazed to see how the strength of those qualities in Josh, Caleb, and Sarah has drawn other people to them. They each gained insight that matured them in ways which prompt many of their peers to seek them out for support and counsel in tough situations. We would not be who we are today without the trial we lived through... and there is much good that has grown out of that for each of us.

Credibility to Share with Others – We all know that when we are suffering, we feel no one else could possibly relate to what we are going through. But... bring in a person in the same situation, and we listen. A person who has lived through suffering as great as mine *can* relate to me. When we come through experiences and survive, we gain credibility to speak to others in the same situations.

Once Caleb's story gained some notoriety in the larger community around the Puget Sound area, I began to hear from other mothers with children coping with brain injuries. The secretary at our high school received calls from several mothers asking to contact me. I was always open to these opportunities to share, so I gave the school permission to relay contact information to me, and I called every mom who asked for a call. I did not always have answers for them, but I was humbled and honored that they would feel safe enough to share their fears and burdens with me, a stranger. Of course, this is why support groups are so helpful. Human beings find unity in commonly shared experiences, and that unity releases us from isolation in suffering and bolsters us up to listen and learn from others who have walked the path ahead of us.

Caleb was placed into several unique opportunities to share his experience with young athletes. For two summers after he graduated from college, he coached at basketball camps in Oregon and Washington where he was asked to relate his story. The players may have initially expected to hear that his credibility to speak grew from his authority as a coach or from his success as a player, but they quickly heard that the power behind his story lay in the sudden loss of his dream to play college basketball and in how he reacted to that loss. Often times when he speaks to a group of students, the room is completely silent. We all know how unusual silence is for a group of middle school and high school students! But Caleb has *earned* the right to speak to them, and they listen. He has gained a platform to inspire young athletes in a way he may not have gained without the injury he sustained. Ironic, but powerful.

No one enjoys suffering. But there *truly* can be powerful positive outcomes resulting from earth-shattering circumstances. The challenge for us as people becomes how we look at and respond to the suffering. Very few positive outcomes can be seen in the midst of facing the barrage of negatives in suffering. We can focus on the loss, pain, fear, and grief; consequently, we may completely miss any good that can grow out of our suffering. But I believe that if we want to truly survive past the pain, we *must* look for the positive. Often times, the good is not obvious. But it *will* be there. So we have a choice. We can keep our eyes narrowly focused on the pain, which may very well be no fault of our own. Or we can look to a broader scope and seek out the good sprouting amidst the suffering. This choice is not easy, but it will be rewarding if we have the faith and the courage to expand our view and consciously pursue the blessings.

Chapter 12

Adjusting to New Goals and Dreams

CR

Caleb and I came home from Children's on the evening of Friday, October 21, 2005. Filled with excitement at this milestone, we packed up all his belongings and drove home for good. We knew we had months of out-patient therapy ahead, but going home felt great!

On Monday, October 24, Mount Si High School held their homecoming assembly. Hoping to jump back into his life as soon as possible, Caleb asked to attend the assembly. I called the high school to inquire about taking him to school for that part of the day. They openly approved his visit. We arrived early so I could get him seated and settled before the other students flooded into the gym. Wanting to stay close and still provide him with some space, I found a safe place to stand in the background. He soaked up the homecoming activities *and* we had a surprise. As homecoming royalty was announced, we heard Caleb's named called as the sophomore prince. It was quite a memorable moment to watch Caleb walk up to receive his royalty sash and to announce the sophomore princess... his own date, Kara.

Caleb was in his element the weekend of homecoming. For our school, Friday night included royalty events and the football game, followed by a homecoming dance on Saturday night. At halftime on Friday, all the royalty was recognized. Caleb's return to school prompted many students to feel a sense of school pride, and as his name was announced, the student section began to cheer "C-Dub, C-Dub". Saturday evening, a group of twenty-two sophomore students gathered to spend the evening together. This group included many friends who had visited and spent hours at the hospitals or in our home over the past four months. Several parents chipped in to rent a big party bus, and all twenty-two students rode to dinner and then to the dance. Caleb had a fabulous time and later commented that it was one of the most wonderful weekends of his whole high school experience.

God continued to give me little windows to see Caleb's improvement along the way. Even seemingly insignificant changes deeply touched me as I watched him through the healing process. One such event came on the Sunday following Thanksgiving, November 27, 2005. As our family sat in church singing the worship songs, I happened to look over and see Caleb singing! Certainly, this may seem small, but to me it was an uplifting moment. Up to this point, he had not retrieved strong enough control over his voice to sing. Although his musical ability would not win any awards, the sound of his deep voice singing offered reason for me to celebrate. Faithfully, God provided moments to testify to His continuous presence and healing hand in Caleb's life.

As Caleb reintegrated back into school, he enjoyed the chance to be back with his friends. Occasionally he seemed reflective; he was keenly aware that he almost lost the chance to go to school, and he appreciated the opportunity to continue his education. Getting back up to speed academically, however, took patience, persistence, and a willingness to be humbled. Before the injury, his name appeared on the honor roll often. As he worked back into high school courses, he faced new struggles. Due to the heavy damage in the language center of his brain, academic assessments showed his reading and writing skills fell around a fourth grade level, which of course impacted his ability to succeed in a variety of classes. I worked closely with administrative and special needs staff as we selected courses with familiar teachers who were willing to mentor him through the reintegration. We felt encouraged that his math skills were still strong, and he was able to enroll in an algebra class with no special accommodations. In order to assist in the transition, Caleb was assigned a special needs aide. Heather was a perfect fit. She had known Caleb since he was in third grade when he played basketball with her son. She accompanied Caleb throughout his day. Her job was to take notes in class when he could not keep up or his hand became fatigued and to discretely follow him from class to class, giving him freedom to interact with others while still watching for situations that may present challenges for his developing mobility. With all this support in place, Caleb enrolled in four courses.

He returned to school in November which is the month that high school basketball gets underway. The senior players of 2006 had developed into a strong team, and although he was two years younger, Caleb had played up with these boys off-and-on since third grade. Many of these seniors loved playing with Caleb because of his court awareness and ability to make remarkable passes. During the summer league games in the weeks before the accident, Caleb and the senior point guard were paired on the court, which presented a formidable challenge to opponents. Consequently, the Mount Si summer league team upset some of the top teams in the Seattle area during those summer league games. We all had realistic hopes that this team would not only qualify for but also be strong contenders at the state playoffs. However, for Caleb... that opportunity was now lost.

Although he could not play, the coach and players included Caleb as a part of the team. At one of the first home games, the coach presented Caleb with a team sweatshirt. Caleb often stayed after school to watch practices and shoot around on free hoops. He attended team dinners, cheered from the stands at home games, and accompanied the team on the bus to away games. Even with the loss of playing on the team, he seemed to truly enjoy participating as much as possible.

As the season progressed, it became apparent that the team would end with a strong winning season and a probable berth at the state playoffs. Mount Si started to draw media attention, and staff at the *Seattle Times* heard about the unusual circumstances surrounding this team. A sports reporter tracked the story and wrote an article on the team and Caleb. Much of the report focused on the way the team rallied around Caleb and dedicated the season to him.

In spite of his side-line status, his presence at practices and in the stands inspired the team. Caleb's picture and story appeared on the front page of the *Seattle Times* sports section on February 14, 2006. Later, Mount Si qualified for the state basketball tournament, and the local *CBS* news affiliate ran a story about Caleb, the team, and the run for state. Again, the coach and team commented on the influence Caleb contributed to their season. The players wrote "CW" on their game shoes and on armbands strapped to their game bags. A short time later, Caleb was awarded the Applebee's Prep Athlete of the Week, so he and the varsity coach were interviewed on a radio talk show. Strangely ironic, we originally expected Caleb to contribute from the court in the success of this season, but instead, he motivated the team just as significantly from the stands.

Feeling a strong desire to support the Mount Si players through this significant season, Andy and I attended several regular season games. We rarely traveled to out-of-town games, but when we did attend the Mercer Island game, we received a warm welcome from many of the opposing players. Like any distinctive community (sports, art, drama, music) existing within a large metropolitan area, participants develop relationships with other members all throughout their local region. Over the years, Caleb's friendships with players from all around the Puget Sound region grew out of mutual respect for one another. Caleb and the Mercer Island boys maintained a special bond due to years of playing competitive basketball not only as opponents but also as teammates. Caleb's injury deeply impacted many of those players, and several of the boys visited the hospital and kept contact with Caleb throughout the recovery.

During the season, Andy and I attended senior night at Mount Si High School in addition to several district playoff games. Although we wanted to support the team and celebrate their success, watching each game and recognizing Caleb's absence inflicted excruciating pain. I often cried after games... sometimes fighting tears in the gym and falling apart on the way home. I clearly remember the pain of senior night as parents joined their sons on the court. We would never experience that. Josh was a senior in 2006, and although he had played basketball in the past, he chose not to play his senior year. Consequently, we would not stand with Josh this year, and we would not stand with Caleb in the future. The night Mount Si won the District playoffs at Bellevue Community College was another tough night. But the absolute worst night followed an early round State Tournament game we attended. I thought I would have the strength to handle the emotions, and I managed well during the game. Mount Si won the game, and Caleb, anxious to stay and watch some other games with the team, found a ride home with another dad. As Andy and I walked out of the Tacoma Dome and to our car, I really fell apart. We had both dreamt about Josh and Caleb playing together at this particular State Tournament, and even though we were happy for the team, we grieved at the personal loss we felt. I cried the whole ride home from the Tacoma Dome... about an hour drive. That was the last game we attended for the year. The season ended with Mount Si winning its first KingCo league championship and finishing sixth at state – Mount Si's most successful appearance at the state tournament since the 1970s.

The rest of Caleb's sophomore year progressed smoothly. As he continued to recover balance, strength, and coordination, Ryan and Nate each worked one or two hours a week to guide Caleb through rehab. The high school graciously helped Caleb transition back into school, and by second semester of his sophomore year, he carried a full class load with five classes. He earned full credit for the four classes he completed in the fall semester, and surprisingly, he remained on track to graduate with his class in 2008. Caleb hoped to finish all his high school credits on time and walk with his own class for graduation, and we all worked hard to help him achieve that goal. As the year wound down, we gratefully enjoyed a more relaxed summer than the one before.

At only one year past the date of the accident, Caleb already showed improvement beyond all expectations. He still had many physical and academic hurdles to overcome, but we were all in a great place considering the past year. Caleb began to look toward new goals and dreams. It was certain that he would not play competitive basketball again. But he still loved the game, and we sought ways to keep in touch with the sport.

During Caleb's junior year, the high school basketball coaching staff changed. Varsity coach Garrick took a job in Spokane, WA. We still knew the JV coach, and he agreed to bring Caleb on as an assistant JV coach. Overall, Caleb liked being part of the team, but his youth prevented him from contributing much as a coach. Caleb and Andy also received certification to referee basketball, and they became part of the Pacific Northwest Basketball Officials Association (PNBOA). Caleb did well reffing, and this became a good part-time job for him. At the end of the season, he attended the awards night for the Mount Si team. Andy and I did not feel comfortable going, so Caleb attended alone. That night, the loss of basketball finally hit him, and he caved in to the deep pain that surfaced. Feeling overwhelming grief that night, he pleaded with us to let him play in one game his senior year. We agonized over his pain, but doubted it was realistic that he could play in a game. The risk was high, and he still had so much healing to do.

In the fall of his senior year, Caleb debated about helping with the basketball program again. Two weeks before tryouts, another coaching change moved the freshman coach into the varsity coach slot. Caleb approached this new coach about assisting with the varsity team, and interestingly, coach Jeff had also thought of asking Caleb to be part of the team. So Caleb again began attending practices, but this time he had a few opportunities to play in the drills and scrimmages during practice. As more and more time lapsed from the injury, Caleb's basketball skills started improving. Although he did not have the quickness he had in the past, his court awareness was still strong.

Around Christmas time, Caleb again asked about playing in one more game. Andy and I talked about it and decided to let Caleb play in the upcoming home game against Mercer Island... as long as the high school coach and athletic director approved. We deliberately chose Mercer Island because of the strong bond between Caleb and the senior Mercer Island varsity players. We knew it would mean a great deal to those boys to be part of the event, *and* we knew they would not play in a way that would pose risk to Caleb. The Mount Si coach and athletic director were very open to the idea, and the Mercer Island coach agreed.

The Mercer Island-Mount Si game was scheduled for January 18, 2008 at Mount Si's gym. Things seemed to be coming together. Caleb let everyone know about the event, and both the Mercer Island friends and the Mount Si boys were very excited about this event. Although Caleb was only allowed to play in the one game against Mercer Island, the coaches asked him to join the team as a regular member, to suit up with the team, and to travel with them for the remainder of the season. Caleb agreed, and he again donned a Mount Si uniform.

Finally, game night arrived. We arrived early as Caleb, Andy, and I all sat for interviews with a reporter for Seattle's *NBC* news affiliate. Before the game, we had the chance to say hello to some of the Mercer Island boys as they presented Caleb with a basketball signed by the players from Mercer Island's varsity team. I think the Mercer boys were just as moved and excited about Caleb's return as any Mount Si player was.

By game time, the stands were packed. Many previous players from Mount Si's 2006 state team returned from college to see the game. Friends and community members who had followed Caleb's story filled the stands. The gym felt electrified with the energy. As Caleb led the team onto the court to warm-up, the fans broke out in loud cheers. The clock buzzer blared indicating the end of warm-ups, and Caleb sat on the bench with the other four starters as he waited to be announced for the game. Over the PA system, player names were announced alternating between Mercer Island and Mount Si players. As the last Mercer Island player was announced, Caleb waited to be the final player announced. The noise level grew, and as Caleb's name sounded out, everyone in the gym, both Mount Si and Mercer Island supporters, stood in a standing ovation. The crowded student section boomed out chanting, "Ca-leb Will-iams".

Caleb ran onto the court to greet the players. First, his own teammates gave him high-fives, and then several of the Mercer Island players greeting him with hugs at center court. Amidst hugs, Evan of the Mercer team handed Caleb two t-shirts with "Welcome Back, Caleb!" on the front and "The MI guys" on the sleeve. In all the excitement, Caleb forgot to shake the hands of referees as is the custom... but the refs understood the significance of the moment. The game referees worked under the PNBOA, the same organization that Caleb worked for. The Mount Si coach honored Caleb by starting him and playing him for six minutes the first quarter and two minutes in the third. Caleb, still awkward from all the residual impact of the injury, did not score a point, but the game was about so much more than scoring. The camaraderie Caleb shared with the Mount Si players, the Mercer Island players, the coaches, the refs, and the friends in the stands became a significant moment of unity for everyone in the gym. Caleb was a shadow of his former self as a player. But... here stood a young man who was told he would never play basketball again. He overcame what seemed like insurmountable odds to even be on the floor... and *that* was the focus of the evening.

A few weeks later, Mount Si hosted the final home game of the season – senior night. Andy and I were to be recognized with Caleb and the other seniors and parents. Two years before, I had grieved that we would never experience this moment. But here we were with the other parents; we were walking out to center court and celebrating the basketball moments of our senior son.

Caleb received one more unexpected honor following this return to the court. A few weeks after the Mercer Island game, Andy and Caleb attended a monthly meeting for the PNBOA refs. Each year, the referee association nominates and votes on candidates for annual "Ambassadors of Basketball" awards presented by the PNBOA. The award recipients include one team, one coach, and one player. During the nominating meeting, one of the refs mentioned Caleb's return to the Mercer game and what an accomplishment that was. Many of the officials remembered officiating Caleb as a player over the previous years. One of the officials stood and nominated Caleb for the player Ambassador award. Caleb felt so honored to be nominated. He only played in one game, but the officials honored his determination and character displayed in the basketball community. The nomination honored Caleb in a way we never expected would come out of the events of the past three years. But in an even more surprising moment, a few weeks later we received an email announcing that Caleb had *won* the award! What an amazing ride over the three years.

Three years after the accident, we looked back on many blessings in Caleb's high school basketball experiences. For two years, he experienced basketball from a coach's perspective and from a referee's perspective. His story was told in Seattle newspapers and news broadcasts. People in the sports world were so inspired by his story and determined grit that he received one of the highest player honors awarded to a player in the Puget Sound area. He still missed the thrill of playing, and I suspect that even with the amazing experiences he enjoyed, he would have traded those experiences for a chance to regain his previous skills. Even so, we all recognized the way God restored basketball to Caleb's life. We thought he lost basketball. Yes, it was different, but it was not lost.

Thankfulness

"...giving thanks always and for everything to God the Father in the name of our Lord Jesus Christ..." Ephesians 5:20 (ESV).

It is interesting to me that this section represents perhaps the most difficult beam I crafted for this book. Throughout this journey, I have experienced moments of great thankfulness. But recently, I listened to a sermon on this verse from Ephesians chapter 5, and it struck me how "unthankful" I am. The words of this verse slice through me, *"always... for everything"*. That is *not* how I am thankful. Thankfulness is a conscious decision for me. It is an exercise and discipline of the will. I am easily thankful for the victories, and I quickly praise and thank God for victories, healing, and growth since the injury. But true thankfulness in the times of fear, uncertainty, and continued struggle – "always and for everything" – eludes me. The long term effects of a brain injury may morph as time passes, but some consequences will *always* be with Caleb in *everything* he faces. Lately, I hear my own prayers of pleading, "Lord, please have mercy. Could Caleb just get a break in _____?" Fill in the blank... whatever is the latest trial, I am *not* thankful for the way the Traumatic Brain Injury consequences impact Caleb's life.

How can I move to being thankful *"always and for everything"*? One thing I realize – this will be a life-long excursion for me. When I feel ungrateful, I must again fall to my knees repenting of my ungrateful heart and my lack of trust in the love and faithfulness of Jesus. Does that seem too harsh? Is lack of thankfulness really lack of trust in Jesus? Yes! My ungrateful heart looks to the world for my security. My ungrateful heart looks to temporal situations as being all important. My ungrateful heart fails to see that eternal consequences far outweigh earthly, temporal consequences. I let myself remain tethered to this world. Cutting that tether leaves me free-falling and uncertain about what the future holds. But cutting that tether will also help me to rely more fully on the eternal tether Jesus longs to give me. And if I am tethered to Him... if Caleb is tethered to Him... what else has to be "fixed" for me to be always thankful? There will be no consequences of the brain injury in heaven. There will be no fear in heaven. All those things that take my eyes off being thankful "*always* and for *everything*" will be insignificant in heaven. I will experience eternal thankfulness!

I have planned to write on thankfulness for a few weeks now. Last night, I again could sense waves of fear and uncertainty covering me. Any seed of thankfulness in my heart began to drown in those fears. Unable to grasp even a mustard seed of thankfulness, I sunk further under the waves of despair in the reality of my unworthiness to write about thankfulness. My dear husband prayed over me. I so appreciate his support and love. I began to feel more peace, but I still perceived the waves crashing all around me.

This morning, I still avoided writing on thankfulness. Of course, I could justify the procrastination... so many *other* tasks needed to take precedence today. As my other tasks wrapped up, I had no excuses left... time to tackle thankfulness. A wondrous thing happened... as I sat typing each word, I began to detect a life preserver pulling me from the choppy waves. A more genuine peace began to shield me from the dangers in the storm. I know the depths I can fall to when I rely on my own power. This rescue came from outside me. That in itself gives me hope... *and* thankfulness.

I will need to be rescued again. Oh, to be able to be thankful "*always* and for *everything*"! But for today, I am experiencing thankfulness.

"The steadfast love of the Lord never ceases; His mercies never come to an end; they are new every morning; great is Your faithfulness" (Lamentations 3:22-23 ESV).

I delight that this verse appears in Lamentations! Even when I lament, He personally showers me in steadfast love and mercy. Today, thankfulness is *not* an exercise of my own will... it is His gift to me!

Chapter 13

Full Circle to Restoration

 C3

Caleb continued to work hard both in school and with his therapies. High school graduation seemed impossible only a few years earlier, but now we prepared for that monumental event. While Caleb hoped to go to college, he still fought an uphill battle in this arena. His high school grades were very good, especially considering what he overcame. But his test scores came back rather low compared to other students. His college options also remained limited as public universities in the state of Washington require a year of high school foreign language, and since Caleb still struggled with verbal skills, taking a foreign language was not realistic. We opted for him to request an interview with admission counselors at the two private universities he considered. After meeting Caleb and hearing his story, both schools sent Caleb acceptance letters. He and I visited both schools, and eventually, we all decided that he would head to Spokane for college.

College is tough for any student, but a Traumatic Brain Injury really raises the level of difficulty. The first week of classes, Caleb called me in tears. He loved where he was, but seriously doubted he could survive the rigors of college. So we stepped back again and set up a "game plan". As he settled into a routine and took one challenge at a time, Caleb made it through his first year. With that first year completed, we started to believe he could graduate. We certainly experienced many more bumps along the way, but we rejoiced in every victory. Caleb called me often with discouragement over low exam scores. Often times, when the class average on an exam hit around eighty percent, his score most likely fell around sixty percent. I started praying for grades to come back with 'C's, and once I even rejoiced over a 'D'. It was a discouraging blow when one final grade showed on his transcript as 'no credit', but that happened only once in his four years. We focused on the big picture and remembered that each passed class moved him closer to the credits necessary for graduation.

As is true for most students, college is about so much more than academics. College offers opportunity to gain independence and mature into adulthood. In his senior year, Caleb had to complete a professional internship. Again, basketball opportunities entered into the mix. Through his out-going personality, he met a contact who knew the founder of Northwest Basketball Camps (NBC). The main offices for NBC are located only a few blocks from the university Caleb attended. After some discussion with the NBC staff, Caleb received an internship with NBC, which he felt was a dream opportunity. Even after his college graduation, he continued to stay heavily involved with NBC basketball programs as he coached summer camps, varsity academies, seasonal clinics, and tournament teams. At the summer camps, Caleb shared his story several times and inspired many teenagers through his positive attitude which was only possible because of a strong faith. Caleb's involvement through NBC provided openings to coach the game he still loves *and* to share a unique story which encouraged young athletes to set goals and work hard regardless of what circumstances bring into life.

During the spring of 2012, we looked forward to the day Caleb would graduate from college. But we again faced hurdles that seemed to thwart his goals. As he struggled with a couple overwhelming class projects, he and I talked on the phone to brainstorm ways he could adequately complete these projects. Fear that he might not pass these courses crept into my mind, and I faced the reality that he may not graduate after all. This thought so disheartened me that I again fell to my knees.

I prayed that all the hard work for Caleb to claw his way through several difficult courses would not end with the disappointment of missing graduation. As the last month of senior year came to a close, all his projects were completed and received passing scores. Graduation became a reality! Words feel inadequate to relate the accomplishment and joy I felt when Caleb *did* pass those final courses. He *did* receive a B.A. in Speech Communication. He *did* walk across the stage on graduation day – of all days, Mother's Day 2012! About six weeks after graduation, we passed the seven year anniversary date of the accident, and Caleb passed that anniversary date possessing a college degree – amazing!

I feel certain we have not yet faced the last storm Caleb will need to navigate, but seeing that college diploma certainly represented a landmark for us all. Seven years earlier, the odds stood harshly against Caleb walking or talking again, let alone finishing high school. Even less likely was the possibility that Caleb could graduate from college. We grieved, struggled, fought, and endured several obstacles along the way. We rejoiced over every small victory... even if that victory fell short of our hopes. A victory still represented forward progress *and* God's faithfulness through each storm. Recently, someone shared with me a thought which struck me with an "ah ha" moment: Life is not about successes. Life is about overcoming. Caleb may not enjoy the successes I dreamed for him, but what has been overcome in his life speaks far more powerfully of success than what I envisioned for him.

Monuments and Memorials

*"Then Joshua called the twelve men from the people of
Israel, whom he had appointed, a man from each tribe.
And Joshua said to them, 'Pass on before the ark of the
Lord your God into the midst of the Jordan, and take up
each of you a stone upon his shoulder, according to the
number of the tribes of the people of Israel, that this may
be a sign among you. When your children ask in time to
come, "What do those stones mean to you?" then you shall
tell them that the waters of the Jordan were cut off before
the ark of the covenant of the Lord. When it passed over
the Jordan, the waters of the Jordan were cut off. So these
stones shall be to the people of Israel a memorial forever'"
Joshua 4:4-7 (ESV).*

Since I lived through a truly remarkable, miraculous
healing of my son, some people might think that I possess
an unwavering trust and faith in God. After all, I saw His
power in a tangible, personal way. I should feel so
intimately confident in His power and care for me that I
never fear again. But I totally relate to the Children of
Israel... those Jews who experienced the miraculous
release from Egyptian slavery. They watched God bring
the Egyptians low with ten impressive plagues of nature.
Each plague escalated in manifesting God's reign over the
created world. By the time the Israelites went into the
wilderness, they should have felt complete confidence in
God's provision. But what happened? They were pinned
against the Red Sea, and their immediate response was
fear. So God obliged and parted the sea to allow His
children to cross. Ah... *Now* they will not fear... But wait!
In the wilderness they have no food and no water. They
could die! Fear rears up again. Patiently, God provided
manna, a special food never seen before and never seen
since. The people received ample manna every morning,

and God brought flocks of quail to the encampment. He caused streams of fresh water to gush from rocks. Remarkable! God provided bread, meat, and water in a desolate desert! Certainly *that* will kill all fear! But wait! The people arrived at the Promised Land. They sent out twelve spies to investigate the people of the land. GIANTS! I can almost hear their thoughts, "Sure, God parted the sea. He provided manna, quail, and water. But we are grasshoppers compared to these giant people!" They succumbed to fear again! But they had lived miracles over and over again. How could they doubt God could and would defeat the giants in the land? They witnessed a God who was big enough to "fix" every trial and enemy they faced... and yet they lacked faith every time a new trial surfaced. I could easily say, "How faithless these people were. I would have shown more faith if I lived the miracles they lived!" But wait! I am *exactly* like those people!

I lived a miracle. God has faithfully broken down barrier after barrier as Caleb has healed and flourished. Yes, flourished! God showed Himself big enough and faithful enough to heal Caleb from a Traumatic Brain Injury. Such a healing goes completely against the expectation of the laws of nature... as do seas parting, bread falling from heaven, and water spewing from rocks. I should have *no* fear... just like the Israelites should have had no fear. But I fear again every time a new "giant" appears – a tough college class, a tough job situation, a memory lapse. I am no different than the children of Israel. In spite of repeated manifestations of God's faithfulness and power, they feared... and so do I. But regardless of my faithlessness, He continues to bless me. When I am faithless, He is faithful.

He knew we humans could not hold onto that faith and trust. He knew we would "forget" His faithfulness. So He instructed the children of Israel to build memorials. In Joshua chapter 4, the people crossed the Jordan River – another miracle when God stopped the river from flowing so the people walked into the Promised Land on dry soil! But this time, they stopped and built a memorial.

They constructed a visual reminder of God's faithfulness. The reminder encouraged not only the present generation but also the generations to come. So I look to my memorials. Here are some of *my* memorials since the accident:

- first chuckle

- first time we ate dinner together as a family

- returning to classes at the high school

- transitioning out of all special needs classes

- graduating from high school

- playing basketball in the back yard with friends

- graduating from college

- coaching basketball

As I write this list, I realize there are too many to include.

When I feel fear creeping up on me, I look back on these memorials. God has been so faithful... and He will continue to be faithful. If I look to my memorials, the fear floats away and peace fills the spaces left open. How do I face giants? Look to my monuments. The monuments dwarf any giant that comes my way.

Chapter 14

Light of Purpose

CR

The past nine years have been a long and difficult ride. To this day, I struggle with moving past the events of that day at the river. Writing this book played a part in my spiritual voyage and personal struggle. *Voyage* accurately depicts the way I often feel. I become "seasick" from being tossed about on the waves of stormy days. I feel the weight of my personal weaknesses and lack of faith. I hear a voice inside saying, "Who are you to write a book about passing through this storm? You still hang on to pain and fear." That voice is right! I do still fight the pain of the event and the fear of what lies ahead. But, this book is not about *my* ability to overcome a storm. This book is about a powerful God who did and still does walk with me through the storm. He gave me (and still gives me) glimmers of light when I was (and am) engulfed in the darkness and huddled in a corner.

Sometimes I must consciously decide to look toward the final two beams of my story: Faith and Acceptance. I often struggle to keep my eyes focused on the light of these two beams. But when I look back and view the memorials of God's faithfulness throughout the gale, I begin to live in the warmth and glow of these beams of light. God does not waste suffering. In the appendix following my story, Caleb has written about his "mindset of blessing". For me, it is *hard* to keep a mindset of blessing regarding Caleb's accident and the consequences that we still face. And yet, I *know* there are many changes in Caleb's life and outlook that are far superior to his life and outlook before the accident. So I remember again... *God does not waste suffering!* Our storm easily could have destroyed me and left me in darkness. But God pierced through the storm with His light. Often times I perceived only flickers in the distance, but in time, those flickers penetrated through the clouds and revealed God's story of hope for us. If our story can encourage others, and you, to look toward the Lord, then our suffering is *not* wasted.

Faith

This verse carried me through the trial of Caleb's accident and is still a life verse for me:

"But now thus says the Lord, He who created you, O Jacob, He who formed you, O Israel: 'Fear not, for I have redeemed you; I have called you by name, you are mine. When you pass through the waters, I will be with you; and through the rivers, they shall not overwhelm you; when you walk through fire you shall not be burned, and the flame shall not consume you. For I am the Lord your God, the Holy One of Israel, your Savior'" Isaiah 43:1-3a (ESV).

People have said to me, "You had such faith during the whole experience. I have asked myself if I would have the faith to get through something like that, the way you did." As I personally reflected on such comments, I asked myself, "How *did* I get through that?" I specifically remember commenting at a women's Bible study a few months before the accident that the one thing I feared my faith could not survive was if something happened to one of my children... then something did happen.

I honestly have to say the faith I felt during that time did not come from me. Many days I felt like a helpless ragdoll with no strength to endure the day. I prayed and cried, but each day I was somehow able to get up and accomplish whatever I had to tackle for that day. That strength came not from me; God gave me what I needed each day – and no more.

When God led the children of Israel through the wilderness, He gave a daily allowance of manna from heaven. The gift of food plentifully fulfilled the needs for the day, but the people were expected to trust God to give provision for tomorrow, and the next tomorrow, and so on. If anyone took surplus, out of fear for tomorrow, the manna rotted and was lost.

The early months after the accident became my "Manna from Heaven" stage of the experience. I did not have the strength to cope with tomorrow... only with today. Tomorrow was too unknown and a fearful place. My prayer became, "Help me to trust that You are still healing until *You* show us differently."

To me this did not feel like some great act of faith... it was an act of survival. If I didn't look to God every day, I possessed no more strength than to crawl into a corner, curl into a ball, go to sleep, and hopefully not wake up. I did not have some great reservoir of faith... my reservoir was filled with fear. I feared Caleb would not wake up, and that if he did, he would not be able to know us or communicate with us. I feared he would never be able to go back to high school let alone college. I feared he could never live on his own. I feared he would never walk again. I feared we had lost his dreams, his abilities, his personality, his humor, his independence... that even if he woke up, he would be so different that the Caleb I had known and loved would be essentially dead and would be replaced by a stranger. My fear and pain reservoir was vast and housed ample supply for me to draw out new fears every day. Only through God's daily, sometimes moment to moment, mercy was I able to turn my eyes away from my own reservoir of fear and draw from His reservoir of hope.

So, now as I look back, I can understand why others may have seen great faith at that time. He knew others (such as Caleb's young friends) needed to see active faith and to observe what trusting God looks like. He graciously provided the means and allowed me to be His conduit of faith.

It would seem that after living through the entire experience I could now draw on a newly formed, immense reservoir of faith and trust. It would seem. But the reality is that my personal default is still fear. Sometimes old fears resurface, and sometimes new and improved fears emerge. Sometimes I feel that I live in a constant state of "waiting for the other shoe to drop".

So now what? My situation remains the same... and may always be the same. I can relate to Paul who suffered from a weakness of body that he asked God to heal. He asked several times, but God would not heal the infirmity. God simply answered,

"'My grace is sufficient for you, for my power is perfected in weakness'" (2 Corinthians 12:9 ESV).

I hate my weakness of fear. Though not quite the same as Paul's bodily weakness, my fear easily morphs into panic and becomes debilitating. It is my thorn. I know fear is actually lack of trust in God. My fear stems out of spiritual infirmity born out of my feeble, sinful flesh. Consequently, I often feel shame and condemnation over my lack of trust.

I know that I have lived through a mighty act of healing: God's remarkable provision to save my child. I believe that God has saved Caleb for a purpose greater than I understand, so won't He also protect Caleb now? I try to rationalize my fear away, but I cannot cure my fear. So, I ask God to remove it because I believe God is powerful enough to remove it. When I pray to Him, I honestly desire freedom from the chains that fear wraps around me. But He doesn't "remove" it; He forces me to cope with it. He answers me, "My grace is sufficient for you, for my power is perfected in weakness."

When I bring my fear to God, He provides the manna of His grace and power to fight my fear for today. I may have to collect manna again in order to overcome the fears of another day. But the manna will again rain from heaven for me tomorrow. Maybe that cycle of daily receiving His spiritual manna is how His "power is perfected". He certainly *could* take my fear away, and I would not have to deal with it again. But in His mercy, He uses even my own self-inflicted weakness to draw me back to Him on a daily basis. My fear drives me to prayer, and then in some paradoxical way, my fear leads me to renewed strength and faith.

It is still possible that God may have a plan to take Caleb to heaven before He takes me. I could still lose Caleb in my lifetime. Caleb does not retain some supernatural force field protecting him from danger just because he has been spared in the past. But I can rely on the opening verses of Isaiah chapter 43. Even as I pass through trials that threaten to drown me, I will not be overwhelmed. Even as I walk through fiery circumstances that threaten to burn me up, I will not be consumed. Faith is not believing I will always have happy endings, faith is believing that God will provide manna, strength, hope, and His presence regardless of the outcome. I do not have to live in fear... I can live in hope and peace.

Acceptance

"And we know that God causes all things to work together for good to those who love God, to those who are called according to His purpose" Romans 8:28 (NASB).

Acceptance is the place I arrive when I move past my earthly fears and believe that God has my good in mind... even if death is part of that good. Many people use Romans 8:28 to comfort those in pain. I love this verse, but it can be terribly misunderstood. All things work together for good for God's people. That does not mean all things that happen are good. Divorce, rape, murder, injustice, abuse, so much more... how can these be good? That is not the point of this verse. Even God hates injustice, abuse, and evil. The point is that God can and will utilize difficult "things" to work good "things". Work is defined as, "activity in which one exerts strength or faculties to do or perform something... a specific task, duty, function, or assignment *often being a part or phase of some larger activity*"[1] (*Merriam-Webster's Collegiate Dictionary* – emphasis added). Did God have any good for Caleb in this accident? I can look back and say a resounding, "Yes!" Caleb is a different person... but that is not bad. He is much more relaxed with who he is. He truly lives each day as a gift. He is much more talkative, and he loves to spend time with people. He lost his dream because of his accident. He lived basketball before the accident – to the point that he felt lost in his purpose after he lost basketball. But the accident has given him new dreams and new goals. These new goals focus much more on making a positive impact on the lives of others. The accident was not "good". What we lived through was not

---

1. By permission. From *Merriam-Webster's Collegiate® Dictionary, 11th Edition* ©2014 by Merriam-Webster, Inc. (www.Merriam-Webster.com)

"good". But through God's work, some larger activity is being accomplished... I don't think we even see yet where it is all going.

But just like coping with my fear, learning to live in acceptance is a spiritual battle. We have a positive story to tell. Caleb came out okay... still with deficit, but remarkably okay. How do people live in faith that God can do a mighty work, but accept that God may not do the mighty work? This is a difficult question. He may act differently than we hope for. This question goes to the same root as the question, "Why does God let bad things happen to good people?" I believe this question will be asked until the end of time. Why? Because it goes to the question of whether God is good and has our good in mind. It pushes me to let God be God. It compels me to admit that it is not my place to judge God. It challenges me to:

- Believe God can heal – Accept He may not.

- Believe God has a plan for my life – Accept it may not be the same plan I have or expect.

- Believe He will give me all I need – Accept His grace is sufficient for what I see as unfilled need.

- Believe He loves me enough to sacrifice His life for me – Accept I may have to sacrifice and suffer loss to receive full life.

I would love to live in a place of acceptance every hour of every day. I don't. I struggle with it daily. Even years after the accident and significant recovery, I ask God, "Couldn't Your purposes for Caleb have been accomplished an easier way? Did he have to experience an injury that will have life-long consequences and life-long struggles? Why does the tool used to shape Caleb have to be so hard?" I do not have all the answers, but I do have the answer that God is always working for Caleb's best. He loves Caleb so much that He will allow whatever it takes to draw Caleb to Himself. A friend reminded me that King David cried out to God... David asked God for relief from trial and injustice. But he always came back to a place of worship... even if the injustice continued. I am moved by Psalm 22 which not only prophesies the death of Christ, but also reflects the anguish of David. David asked why and poured out his heart:

"My God, my God, why have You forsaken me? Why are You so far from saving me, from the words of my groaning? O my God, I cry by day, but You do not answer, and by night, but I find no rest... I am poured out like water, and all my bones are out of joint; my heart is like wax; it is melted within my breast; my strength is dried up like a potsherd, and my tongue sticks to my jaws; you lay me in the dust of death" (Psalm 22:1-2, 14-15 ESV).

But David praises God even in the midst of the suffering. Through praise and worship, David remembers that God is for him.

"You have kept count of my tossings; put my tears in Your bottle. Are they not in Your book? Then my enemies will turn back in the day when I call. This I know, that God is for me. In God, whose word I praise, in the Lord, whose work I praise, in God I trust; I shall not be afraid. What can man do to me?" (Psalm 56:8-11 ESV).

David receives strength from recalling God's faithfulness.

"I will tell of Your name to my brothers; in the midst of the congregation I will praise You; You who fear the Lord, praise Him! All you offspring of Jacob, glorify Him, and stand in awe of Him, all you offspring of Israel! For He has not despised or abhorred the affliction of the afflicted, and He has not hidden His face from him, but has heard, when he cried to Him" (Psalm 22: 22-24 ESV).

If I can come to the place of acceptance - believing God has my good in mind – then I can worship. And if I worship – even when I feel I cannot – I will be moved to accept. I too will learn to accept what Job accepted: God is good; God is for me; God is worthy to be praised.

Appendix

CR

As time has passed, Caleb has journeyed through his own personal struggles to accept and to move on from the consequences of his injury. In spite of his challenges, Caleb's attitude has remained quite positive through most of the experience. He views failures as opportunities; he understands leadership requires humility; he values relationships above circumstances; and he chooses to keep a positive outlook on life. These perspectives can only be explained as gifts from God. Relying solely on human nature limits the ability to maintain a positive outlook through adversity. It is only through keeping a strong spiritual focus that people can remain truly optimistic. We hope that Caleb's own words will bring encouragement and strength for others to see life from a "glass is half full" perspective.

Appendix A

A Beam for Caleb: Achievement Grows from Failure

CR

Coming to understand and accept the consequences of my brain injury revealed a hard road. While at Children's Hospital going through rehab, I expected to work hard and eventually be the person I was before. I completely anticipated gaining back all my physical abilities. But as I ventured down the road to recovery, I began to realize that I must deal with loss.

One night in particular, the realization of my condition fully hit me. Many times when people visited me at the hospital or at home, they told me how gifted I was as a basketball player. Because I did not fully understand the total impact of my injury, I figured I would get right back into basketball once my body "healed". I believed that hard work would naturally allow me to gain back my skills on the court. One Saturday, my mom and I returned home from Children's Hospital for a weekend. As my family ate dinner together, I began to snap at others due to the underlying fear and anger which suddenly overwhelmed me. It was not like me to direct cruel words at people; yet as the reality hit, and I struggled to deal with the painful feelings rising up, lashing out was exactly what I was doing. My parents sent me to my bedroom. My room was filled with Michael Jordan posters, as well as all of the trophies I had won as a basketball player. I lost it. I broke down in tears for a long period of time. Because of my brain injury, my memory was greatly impacted, and I retained little memory of being the outstanding player others described to me. I knew that I had been a very strong player, but at the time, I had absolutely no recollection that I was a top ranked player in the Pacific Northwest region. This loss of memory made it even tougher for me to accept what I faced that night.

The combination of hearing each compliment of my abilities and also hearing the reality of the seriousness of the injury I had sustained was too much. I felt filled with questions and uncertainty. What other areas of my life had I forgotten? That night (and even to this day) my mind was void of any memory related to the day of my accident at Blue Hole on the Snoqualmie River. What was going through my thought process prior to falling? Could I have acted differently to prevent falling off the rope? As my brain fought to remember and process what had happened to me, I felt overwhelmed. I even lacked the ability to truly understand what had taken place. After a period of time, my parents joined me, only to find me in tears. As we talked, I shared the feelings I was struggling with. That night ended with a limited understanding of what doctors had been telling my parents, "Caleb should not, and most likely will be unable to, play basketball ever again." This tore me apart. I faced the choice either to accept what the doctors predicted of my future or to discover for myself what I could and could not do. I was not willing to accept their assessment. Looking back, I believe that night sparked a fire in me to get to work on recovering, regardless of the obstacles.

Regaining the ability to play the sport of basketball presented a long road to travel, but I saw no reason not to strive toward that goal. I had a strong team of people continually encouraging and supporting my recovery, so it was then up to me to push my limits. Improving my balance, strength, and coordination required my persistence through many difficult hours of workouts that were developed by my personal trainers. In addition to regaining my physical strength and coordination, I had to reclaim the ability to process, think, and reason.

Mental recovery included practicing numerous word games and strategy games, talking through various situations, and completing mind-strengthening exercises. Building skills and abilities necessitated a great deal of practice, a strong work ethic, and most importantly... failures.

Failure is a paradox because people hate to fail, and yet, failure allows a person to learn valuable lessons and to grow. In my situation of recovery through therapy and life in general, failures were building blocks of progress toward healing. Each failure I experienced revealed ineffective methods for reaching a particular task, which then led me to effective ways to achieve the goal. This mindset greatly differs to what is commonly seen in today's society. The "normal" response to failure can be extremely degrading and ultimately defeating to the person or group who failed. Society tends to view failure as a sign of hopelessness with no hint of achievement. This, in turn, causes an individual to give in and be conquered by the failure. When we view failure as a stepping stone, failure no longer has victory over us; rather, we have victory over failure.

Sometimes when I failed, doubt weighed on me because of my inability to perform a particular task. Each time I failed at a specific task during my recovery, I was built up with words of encouragement and constructive (not destructive) criticism from my trainers. Being a competitive person who was accustomed to succeeding, I used each word of correction and of encouragement to push myself harder. Failures became one of the most important tools in my recovery. Every instance of failure better equipped me with the ability to grow and to improve. Being afraid of failure was the exact same thing as being afraid of growth. In no way was I ever going to recover and grow without the determined attitude to accept failure. The viewpoint I took in many instances was that I had absolutely nothing gained if I was to avoid trying. Completing a task inadequately ultimately brought me one step closer to figuring out how to properly perform the task. Quitting and refusing to work in times of my failures would have led to a pessimistic mentality, while accepting each failure as a motivator instilled a mindset of growth.

At first, I felt defeated that I may have lost the ability to ever play the sport of basketball again. If I had allowed defeat to control me, reclaiming even some of my ability would have been impossible. I may not be the same player I was before the injury, but because I was willing to risk failure during rehab, I gained back the ability to play with competitive players. I learned to accept the skills I could recover and to work hard at improving those skills to the best of my new capabilities. Not only did I gain back a chance to play, but by being willing to look beyond my past experiences, I gained some new opportunities. Coaching and reffing basketball broadened the scope of my basketball experiences, and I might have missed those had I given in to my limitations. It was worth risking failure to discover new successes. Previously, I was driven by the challenge to be the "best" player on the floor. That same drive still exists in me; however, I now focus on the comradery I experience on the court and on the ways I coach in order to instill those higher values in young players.

Appendix B

A Beam for Caleb: Focusing on Others Through Leadership

ᙓ

Ever wonder why certain people in life seem to be "natural born leaders", while others will always be labeled as the "followers"? Leadership is not exactly a character trait a person is just born with, and neither is it something which can be mastered through reading a textbook. Is a public speaker who can fluently captivate his/her audience automatically labeled as a leader? Is a pastor of a mega church a perfect leader? There are so many paths an individual can travel to become a leader, but an effective leader may be created through an array of life experiences.

Enduring a severe TBI has allowed me to learn numerous lessons relating to leadership, although I gained leadership tools prior to falling at Blue Hole. During my childhood, playing the game of basketball taught me a variety of lessons. Achieving success in a sport requires a handful of individual attributes and abilities, yet even an athlete who possesses an incredible level of talent may not ever achieve full potential without a team. Basketball teams are comprised of players of all sorts of talent, who rely on a coach as the driving force. The best basketball team has players who can follow the leadership of a coach.

Learning from and observing the leadership qualities of my coaches over the years allowed me to develop my leadership skills on a team. As a point guard, my role on the team was to be a court leader performing the game plan of the coach. This implied that I would show a high level of loyalty to my coach since it was my job to execute whatever the coach expected of the team. A point guard must respect the authority above him/her and not become caught up in receiving his/her own recognition. In many instances, leaders become power hungry, which ultimately destroys any hope of effectively leading a team. Whether in basketball, or any other sport, the moment when an individual player climbs up on a pedestal and desires all recognition coincides with the moment that team chemistry and continuity disappears. The leader of a team may or may not be the best talent on the team, but in either case, the leader needs to be the player who consistently encourages others, follows the coach's leadership, refuses to quit working, and maintains an attitude of team oriented leadership.

Being a leader is often times difficult and forces an individual to push beyond personal comfort levels. The best leaders are able to place personal issues aside and direct their sole focus on achieving the team goal. Some leaders have a gift of influencing and leading others by simply opening their mouths and providing verbal leadership, while other leaders rely on leading through action. Point guards must be able to incorporate both of these leadership styles. Some people perform best when they are told what to do, some respond well to being shown how to accomplish a task, while others may need a combination of both. This relates to my spiritual walk. It is important for me to submit to the authority of Jesus. Sometimes Jesus expects me to be vocal about my faith and sometimes to lead by example. The ways He asks me to lead may not always be easy. Sometimes He pushes me to lead in ways that are outside my comfort zones.

The true keys of powerful leadership are keeping a humble attitude and valuing other people. Although a high level of athletic ability is not mandatory for a basketball team leader, it certainly helps. However, becoming successful will naturally draw attention from others and bring higher expectations. Many people are quick to offer respect and favoritism to leaders who win. Winning is great, but it is important to watch whether the leader is leading and performing in a manner which is even worthy of such respect. Real leaders have a humble attitude and are quick to shift all credit of success to their teammates. Every team has a player or two who do not receive much playing time due to various reasons; however, an effective leader is able to utilize these players' strengths and make them a valuable aspect of the team. Leaders earn true respect when they value their teammates' successes more than their own. A leader who portrays a humble attitude and invests in the success of others is the leader who will be followed.

As a basketball player, I had been coached by my dad to develop those attributes of humble leadership that promote the success of other teammates. I knew that my role as point guard was to set up opportunities for my teammates on the court. My job was to see potential in each teammate and to do my best to draw out that potential. Once my competitive playing days of basketball came to an abrupt halt, the leadership skills I learned while playing this game would continue to be evident in the new areas of my life. Throughout my recovery and new experiences after the injury, I was able to see how leadership filters into most avenues of life.

Following the instruction of my therapists taught me how they lead patients to push toward recovery. At times, having to follow the instruction was difficult... extremely difficult and even demoralizing. These therapists constantly gave me challenges which pushed me to my limit in a very similar way that my basketball coaches had pushed me as a point guard. There were times where I "failed" to accomplish a task presented to me, but as strong leaders, my therapists never stopped encouraging me to push on. Their leadership helped me to eventually achieve the task. A successful leader understands how to appropriately address each team member with challenges and opportunities that help the person improve and grow. Each therapist used a unique approach in order to effectively establish a trustworthy relationship with me and push me to reach my full potential. Their therapy styles exemplified excellent qualities of an effective leader: a person who knows how to bring out the best in others.

Ever since my life altering accident, I have developed a much broader view of effective leadership. The "post-accident" version of Caleb is no longer a star basketball player or a 4.0 student, nor is he seen as a standout "winner" from a worldly perspective. Nevertheless, real leadership does not ask for those things anyway. I am inspired by the approach John Quincy Adams, the sixth U.S. President, understood about leadership , "If your actions inspire others to dream more, learn more, do more and become more, you are a leader." This attitude prompts me to be a servant leader. Jesus gave the perfect example of a servant leader. He humbly demonstrated compassion for others as He gently taught them how to grow. My belief about leadership grows out of that model. From the outset, the goal of proper leadership is not to better oneself but to exhibit a passion to positively impact the lives of others. That passion must be based on serving others, which in turn pushes the leader to be humble, compassionate, supportive, encouraging, and valuing when interacting with others, even when people are hard to work with. Jesus Christ saved my life and has continually shown me that the most vital characteristic of a leader is the desire to focus on others.

Appendix C

A Beam for Caleb: Love

 C₃

The word *love* implies various meanings in our society today. In one instance, a person can claim that they just love a specific type of candy bar, and then five minutes later the same person may speak in regards to the amazing love shared with a spouse. The same word, love, obviously has two completely different underlying implications when comparing a candy bar to a spouse. While claiming to "love" an inanimate object has become common in our lives today, the true origin and definition of love became increasingly clear to me throughout my injury and the recovery period of my life. The very existence and ability to love, and be loved, originates perfectly from our Lord and Savior, Jesus. Living each day with the ability to walk, communicate, function, and simply live continually shows me evidence of an unconditional love from Jesus. Extending His love to us, Jesus also provides the ability to give and receive the incredible gift of human love. My life was significantly changed not only through the love of Jesus but also through the gift of love from friends and family.

Numerous instances of love displayed from friends and family filled the summer of 2005 and continued throughout the following years. If I recall correctly, one of my very first memories after waking from my coma was being visited by five of my friends while at home in my hospital bed. McKenzie, Katie, Katelyn, Dennae, and Tana had just finished their league soccer game and chose to visit me following their game. Due to the state I was in, all I could do was lie in my bed and talk briefly with the girls. Everyone wanted to capture an image of this moment as the five surrounded the bed and posed for a picture. The girls all held up the "peace" sign with their fingers and had huge smiles as I attempted to imitate their pose. My smile was one of a boy who hadn't quite gained the muscle control to fully smile, but what stands out in my memory of this moment is the genuine love and friendship each person showed me. I have been asked all types of questions relating to my recovery and abilities following my brain injury, but one question I never hesitate to answer with certainty, "What gave you the motivation to continue pushing yourself in your recovery?" Without a doubt, the constant support and love shown to me by friends, family, and even strangers, gave me daily motivation to continue working towards a possible recovery.

As a fifteen year old male, relearning the "simple" functions of life was often humbling and difficult for me to cope with. Even when I became frustrated and saddened at the situation I was in, the acts of love from others never ceased. Unconditional love is just that, love which is not scared or tainted due to a change of circumstance or future reward. Dozens of my friends sacrificed time out of their summer to visit the hospital, complete housework for my parents, raise money to cover my medical expenses, or pray for healing. Throughout the summer of 2005, my condition rarely changed to any great extent, which could normally result in decreased support from others. What is truly incredible to me is that the high degree of love shown to my family and me never lessened, but rather, it stayed consistent or magnified. During the five weeks I was at Harborview Medical Center in Seattle, the list of visitors surpassed 100 people. This in itself is remarkable. Once I regained awareness of my surroundings, it seemed as if I always had people around me. Although my friends and family had no obligation to spend time with me, they never stopped. Every day at Children's Hospital, I was blessed with the company of friends and family. Each morning and afternoon was filled with intensive therapy, which presented its share of challenges. The highlight of my day was from 6:00 p.m. to 9:00 p.m. when visitors were welcome to spend time with my mom and me. Some days I did not know ahead whether any friends planned to come visit, but each night my mom and I were joined by two or more visitors. This social interaction gave me motivation for the next day when I had to fight through struggles or setbacks. That summer was filled with devastating times for many of us; however, the acts of love provided hope and blessing.

To describe each event and act of service would require an entire book in itself, but there are a few memories which will always be dear to me. September 25, 2005 was my final day at home prior to spending four weeks at Children's Hospital for therapy. That Sunday at church, the pastor invited me up to the front to pray over me. With assistance from my parents, I stepped out of my wheelchair and awkwardly walked to the front. My pastor placed his hands on me and spoke with me. Instantly, every person in the congregation joined around us and began praying for me. Regardless of the likelihood of my recovery at that point in time, the Lord's comfort and love were shown to my family and me through the people surrounding us. That afternoon, my parents hosted a barbeque open to any of my friends. Over forty people chose to spend their Sunday afternoon at our house. Each friend had a huge smile as I was able to interact and converse with them. The next day, I would go to Seattle for my therapy, but my full focus was on this opportunity to spend time with my great friends. At one point during the barbeque, my brother, Josh, and my friend, Remo, helped me walk onto our basketball court. It had been over three months since the last shot I attempted. With the hoop lowered to about seven feet, Remo handed me the basketball as Josh held onto me to support my balance. After a few unsuccessful attempts, I finally made a shot as friends cheered me on. Considering that I was bed-ridden just a month prior to this day, making a basketball shot was a huge accomplishment. Without love, encouragement, and support from Josh and Remo, this memorable experience would not have been possible. The entire day, I felt encouraged by the love expressed to me.

My high school's homecoming week began a few days after my return home from in-patient rehab at Children's Hospital. The school invited me to attend the homecoming royalty assembly where I received quite a gift. I arrived at the school and was helped to a seat next to my friends. As the royalty selection results were revealed at center court, I heard my name announced, and the gym exploded with excitement. Without even knowing if I would be physically able to attend the homecoming game and dance, my classmates and friends voted for me as their class prince. I was also gifted with the opportunity to announce the class princess, Kara, who was my date for the dance. That Saturday night, twenty-one of my friends and I had a blast at dinner and the dance. It was such a blessing to be with each friend as we laughed and enjoyed the opportunity to all be together again.

During the winter of my senior year at Mount Si, I was given the opportunity to act as a student-coach with the varsity basketball team. That January, I was also given the incredible opportunity to play in one actual game. This game was not intended to be defined by the level of skill I displayed or by whether we won, but rather by the chance to play with and against some dear friends. On Friday night, January 18, 2008, Mount Si High School hosted Mercer Island High School, allowing me to play one final high school basketball game against players who were my close friends. I had strong ties with many of the Mercer players because I had played on teams both with and against them. During the summer of my accident, many of the Mercer players visited me at Harborview Medical Center. Now, being on the same court with those players was a miracle. As I sat in the bleachers waiting for the JV game to finish, I was surprised by a great act of love. My good friend, Remo, flew back from college in Iowa just to be there to watch me play. I had no idea he was coming, but I was thrilled to have him there. Of course, I was excited to play a game again, but the people involved with the event were the true focus of this special occasion.

As our team gathered in the locker room before the game, coach informed us that he placed me into the starting lineup. We exited the locker room and ran onto the court for warm-ups. The stands were already full, and as the team appeared, the crowd began chanting "Ca-leb Will-iams". So many emotions ran through my head as I tried to stay focused on making the simple lay-ups. Starting lineups began as I sat patiently on the bench awaiting my call. Each of the other nine players from both teams was announced, making me last up. The announcer began to say, "And making a special..." when every person in the gym stood up and applauded. I ran onto the center court to be greeted by my Mercer Island friend, Evan, who presented me with t-shirts reading "Welcome Back Caleb!" and "The MI guys". It was obvious that this game was not about fierce competition, but about great friendships. The opening tip went up and the game was played. Beyond the outcome of the basketball game itself, that night represented the love and support shown over the past three years. Friends, family, old teammates, past coaches, and news reporters packed the Mount Si gym, and it will be an event I will always cherish.

The years of recovery and growing up with a TBI have contained plenty of challenges, yet the people who supported and loved me through every circumstance motivated me through each step of recovery. The Lord places people into our lives at specific moments, and I am continually thankful for being blessed with amazing people in my life. My own definition of love has been largely shaped over the past nine years of my life, as I have had the privilege of connecting with many incredible people. True love is not rattled by some freak circumstance or challenging condition, but rather remains consistent, and even grows, during the hard times of life. Love is a gift we are privileged to share as we strive to better the lives of others. In selfless expressions of love to others, we also bring glory to the Creator who has given us the greatest love possible.

Appendix D

A Beam for Caleb:
A Mindset of Blessing

ଔ

The past decade of my life has prompted various responses in me ranging from amazing, interesting, weird, miraculous, tragic, depressing, or exciting. Experiencing a Traumatic Brain Injury can easily be viewed as a curse on my life. Few people would ever consider a TBI as a "blessing" for a person, but does that automatically classify this injury as a curse? The view I, or any other person, choose to hold on such an injury is entirely based on mindset. It is so easy for people to place attention on the negatives of a situation without ever stopping to realize the positives and blessings which take place through the particular event. As I progressed through my recovery stages, I faced physical and mental disabilities including struggles to walk, to eat independently, to talk clearly, to process information at my age level, and to understand social situations. Now a decade later, I am a college graduate with restored physical and mental abilities. Throughout my traumatic experience and the years following, I was privileged enough to experience valuable lessons and gain a new perspective on life.

Prior to June 20, 2005, the majority of my life revolved around building my skill and ability to play the game of basketball. Basketball was my passion, and the Lord gifted me with a high degree of athleticism and talent for the game. Many predicted I would go on to play basketball at a Division 1 or 2 university, and I had no doubt in my mind that I would reach that goal. In order to excel at the game, I developed skills of leadership, teamwork, discipline, persistence, and focus. Unknowingly, skills learned through basketball also prepared me for the trial I would face and for the rest of my life. I applied the principles of commitment and hard work, strength of a united team, and strategies for accomplishing goals as I worked through the different stages of my recovery.

Life in America is fast-paced and filled with the idea that we "deserve" things. This mindset can prompt people to take many aspects of life for granted. The capabilities to walk, run, jump, communicate, think, reason, etc. are viewed as "simple" accomplishments. When taking these things for granted as the "norm", it becomes natural to become upset and irritated when things don't turn out exactly as planned and expected. Things as simple as missing a shot in a basketball game or getting a 'B' instead of an 'A' on an exam can completely rock someone's world. Yes, there are appropriate times for people to be upset and disappointed, but these disappointments should not make or break life. There are plenty of difficulties a person faces in life, but to be overtaken by disappointment and anger when goals are not achieved and circumstances do not run as planned only causes a person to live with a negative attitude in life. Remaining focused on negative situations draws people's attention solely to the dark and gloom in life, which consequently, causes people to miss the positives in life. My brain injury has definitely been harmful and has brought some negatives to my life. However, I can see positive change in the perspectives I hold. I would argue that my injury sparked a healing of my point of view.

In our culture, the gift of strong friendships is often overlooked and underappreciated. Before the injury, my focus was in no way wrong, but I allowed my focus of basketball to take my perspective off a few other important areas of life. My traumatic experience shifted my life priority from basketball and athletic ability, and in a way, knocked some sense into my head (no pun intended) in order to see that the people in my life are what truly matters. Relationships with other people now take center stage in my life. All during the summer of my accident, my faithful friends voluntarily gave time and energy to assist me and my family. Many students helped with yard and house work at my home; a group of parents organized a prayer group for my healing; my home community held an auction in order to raise money for my medical bills; friends visited me every day; my basketball team wore my name on their team shoes; my friends created, wore, and sold fund-raiser wrist bands saying "Cdub is my hero" and "I love Caleb". These are only some of the amazing things people did not only for me but also for my family. Basketball and athletics are great and amazing gifts; yet, in no way do these things compete with the gifts of friendship and love from friends and family.

Sometimes the process of a blessing is achieved through hard situations. To be honest, sometimes the process sucks. But the ultimate goal is worth it; and in the end, that "hard" blessing offers the best way for us to grow. As humans, we rely mostly on our own perspectives. But in reality, we only see a small percentage of the overall perspective. Normally, we humans view every bad circumstance as a curse. Due to our limited perspective and understanding, our view of blessing has been distorted to see only good as blessings. But God can see our entire lives and the entire perspective. Therefore, something that seems negative in our lives at a particular point in time may very well be one of the best things that will happen to us. God may have something better in store for us, but we don't always see the big picture of how He uses both good and bad to help us become who He wants us to be. Faith is trusting that God sees the whole perspective and that He will use even bad situations to bring blessings into our lives. There are still many hard obstacles I deal with because of my injury, and some of those hard circumstances will never go away. Sometimes I find it tough to keep trusting. But I choose to have faith that God did use and is still using my traumatic injury to form me more into the person He intends for me to be. By keeping a mindset of faith that God is shaping me, I can see my injury as a blessing and feel confident in the words of the following verse:

"For I know the plans I have for you, declares the Lord, plans for welfare and not for evil, to give you a future and a hope" Jeremiah 29:11 (ESV).

Appendix E

Pictures

CR

- Two pictures about eight weeks after his injury

- Five soccer friends visiting

- Waving to the crowd at the Mount Si stadium dedication

- Friends at the Mount Si football stadium dedication

- Friends at a barbecue

- Shooting hoops

- Friends visiting at Children's Hospital

- Homecoming dance with twenty-two friends

- Rescuers

- Announced for the starting line-up

- Competing again

- Senior night for Mount Si basketball

- Graduating from college

- Family picture

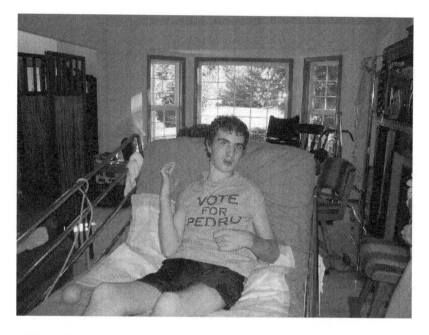

This photo and the one on the next page were the first photos taken after the accident. I could not bear to take any pictures at the hospital. When I considered taking photos, it felt morbid to save images of that uncertain time when Caleb could die.

When these photos were taken, Caleb was still in a coma but was beginning to track us with his eyes.

August 2005

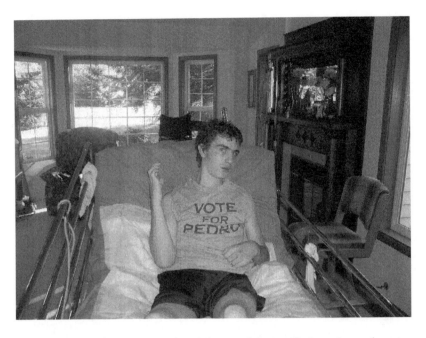

Caleb's right arm was in this position all the time due to the muscle and nerve spasticity.

In the early years after his recovery, Caleb did not like seeing this photo - it bothered him to see himself in this state. Now, as an adult, he can appreciate how much progress he has made and how this image is a reminder of God's mercy to miraculously heal him.

August 2005

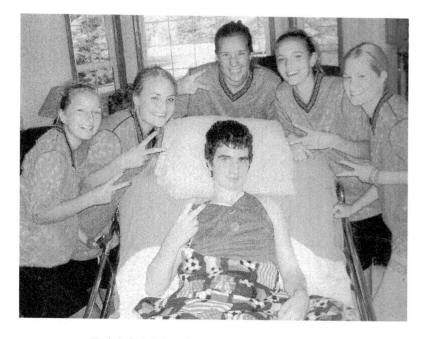

Faithful friends came to visit Caleb
after a soccer game.

From left to right:
McKenzie, Katie, Katelyn, Dennae, and Tana

September 2005

Caleb attended the Mount Si High School stadium dedication. Though unable to master facial expressions, Caleb waved to the crowd as they welcomed him with a standing ovation.

September 23, 2005

Tana and Dennae joined Caleb at the Mount Si
High School stadium dedication. At the time,
this was the best smile Caleb could give.

September 23, 2005

Many friends visited at the barbecue before Caleb
went to Children's Hospital for rehab.

Front left to right: Tana, Caleb, and McKenzie

Middle left to right: McKenzie, Dennae,
Lauren, Michaela, Max, and April

Back left to right: Baker, Kevin, Katelyn, Remo,
Blake, Wes, Ben, Jake, and Justin

September 25, 2005

Remo and Josh helped Caleb shoot a basket at
the barbecue before Caleb went to
Children's Hospital for rehab.

September 25, 2005

Friends regularly visited Caleb at Children's Hospital.
From left to right: Kevin, Corrin, Dennae, and Ben
October 2005

Twenty-two sophomore friends attended homecoming.

Front left to right: Nicole, Katie, Tana, Dennae,
McKenzie, Mariah, Kara, Mikaela, Kyleen, Cailee, Corrin
Back left to right: Ben, Max, Sam, Baker, Blake, Jake,
Caleb, Wes, Ian, Chris, Kevin

October 2005

Our local newspaper followed the story closely.
When Caleb returned to school, they ran this photo of
Caleb and the five boys that rescued him sharing
a hearty laugh outside the high school.

Back left to right: Josh, Justin, and Blake

Front left to right: Ben, Caleb, and Wes

November 2005

(Photo by Sarah Haas)

Caleb jogged onto the court when introduced for the
starting line-up in the Mount Si - Mercer Island game.

January 18, 2008

(Photo by Jim McKiernan)

Caleb and Evan competed during the first quarter
of the Mount Si – Mercer Island game.

January 18, 2008

(Photo by Jim McKiernan)

We celebrated senior night for Mount Si basketball.

February 2008

(Photo by Jim McKiernan)

We celebrated Caleb's college graduation on,
of all days, Mother's Day!

May 13, 2012

A recent family picture with all five of us!

December 2013

Acknowledgements

CR

To the boys who saved Caleb
Justin Poth, Blake Hepner, Ben Emerson, Wes Burdulis, and Joshua Hendricks – you are my heroes! A big hug to you all. Words cannot express well enough our gratitude... but THANK YOU!

To our Lierman and Williams families
You have truly walked this journey with us from the first day at Harborview. You came quickly and often, and you jumped in to help with the hard things that could easily have made you fear and cringe. You saw and heard the worst of our pain and the worst of Caleb's injuries. You stood by us with honest counsel and kept us looking to Jesus for strength. You never tired, even when we did. We love you all.

To the "helper" team who
consistently took shifts to care for Caleb
You were invaluable to me and were the means to give me rest. You also provided moral support in your faithfulness to come week after week (many of you driving long distances to do so) and in your words of encouragement to me each time you came.

To the *many* teens, parents,
and community members
You rallied around us providing support for Joshua and Sarah, cleaning our home, maintaining our yard, visiting Caleb regularly, installing shower bars, building wheelchair ramps, praying for us all, organizing and attending fund-raisers, and many more acts of kindness. The list of names could fill several pages; know that each of your acts of kindness are cherished.

To the medical professionals
(doctors, nurses, therapists)
who took personal interest in Caleb's case
Several of you are friends who stood with us to "interpret"
the barrage of medical information we were processing
early on. You encouraged, counseled and trained us so
that we could care for Caleb. Several of you we met
through the crisis, but you became dear to us and to
Caleb. Our thanks to you all.

To the families, board members, and
teachers at Legacy Homeschool Center
Thank you for working with me so I could continue
teaching even through the recovery process. Names of
people who prayed and supported us, again, would fill
many pages; you were the voice of the Spirit crying out to
God on our behalf.

To the people of Calvary Chapel North Bend
Our gratefulness for your prayers cannot be overstated.
You were also the voices of the Spirit crying out for us.
Thank you for the food and visits that were the hands and
feet of Jesus to us.

To the friends from the Key Peninsula
Your prayers, song composition, and friendship buoyed
us up. You drove a great distance to minister to Andy at
the hospital, and you rallied around him at the yearly
"guys retreat". You included us in gatherings, even to the
point of making the long trek to our home for the annual
summer gathering in order for us to be a part of the event.
You prayed over Caleb on several occasions, standing in
the gap for us. You gathered around us like family and
we are grateful.

To the administrators, teachers, coaches,
students, and staff at Mount Si High School
We are grateful for your support that permitted Caleb to
get back on track with classes. Thank you for allowing for
creative ways to get him back into athletics in the high

181

school and for inventive scheduling which enabled him to graduate on time with his class.

To the administrators, teachers, coaches,
and staff at Snoqualmie Middle School
You encouraged and supported Caleb in his recovery. But you also stood with Sarah in a very difficult time. Our thanks to you.

To the people of Snoqualmie Valley
You supported us through fund-raisers. You honored Caleb by recognizing him as the "Grand Marshall" for the 2006 Festival at Mount Si. You cheered him on at the Mercer Island/Mount Si basketball game his senior year. As a community, you rallied around us, and we will always be grateful.'

To the rescue workers who
cared for Caleb at the river
You did what was necessary to keep Caleb alive and give him a fighting chance. Thank you for your willingness to put your lives on the line for others.

To the teammates, coaches, referees, friends,
and family from the basketball community
We know for many of you, it was very difficult to see someone completely taken out of the game, yet you never forgot him. You kept him connected to the game he loves, and you inspired him in his recovery.

To the owners and staff of
Mt. Si Sport and Fitness
You adopted Caleb as one of your own. Your ongoing support through membership, training, and therapy helped him believe he could recover his physical strength. You pushed the athlete in him to resurface, and you are dear friends.

To my Sarah

You have been my prayer warrior through many rough patches. You were a critical pair of eyes to read pages and pages of copy and provide knowledgeable feedback. God has developed in you strength and beauty. I love you with all my heart!

To my Caleb

Your personal courage and trust in Jesus challenges me to follow Him without fear. You never give up; you always believe that God will provide a way through trial. God has blessed you with the ability to accept His will in your life even when life feels overwhelming. I love you with all my heart!

To my Joshua

You are my steady rock and protector, regardless of circumstance. When I am in very low places, you bolster me up and help me find perspective. God has given you powerful inner strength which fosters deep trust. You always have my back. I love you with all my heart!

To my Andy

You are my balance. You supported me through this whole project by believing in me even when I was not sure I could write this story. You jumped in to help with the tasks that fell outside my abilities (*anything* requiring use of technology ☺). You faithfully stand with me through every circumstance life throws at us. I love you with all my heart!!

Index of Old Testament Scripture Verses

CR

Index of New Testament
Scripture Verses

CR

Purchasing a Copy

ℭℛ

To purchase a copy of this book,
please visit Amazon.com.

If you are interested in an author interview
or a speaking engagement,
contact:

GracefulScript@comcast.net

Made in the USA
Charleston, SC
28 November 2016